THE
PEACE

Also by Roméo Dallaire

Shake Hands with the Devil: The Failure of Humanity in Rwanda
(with Major Brent Beardsley)

They Fight Like Soldiers, They Die Like Children:
The Global Quest to Eradicate the Use of Child Soldiers
(with Jessica Dee Humphreys)

Waiting for First Light: My Ongoing Battle with PTSD
(with Jessica Dee Humphreys)

THE
PEACE

A WARRIOR'S JOURNEY

ROMÉO
DALLAIRE

with JESSICA DEE HUMPHREYS

RANDOM HOUSE CANADA

PUBLISHED BY RANDOM HOUSE CANADA
Copyright © 2024 Roméo Dallaire

www.penguinrandomhouse.ca

Random House Canada and colophon are registered trademarks.

Library and Archives Canada Cataloguing in Publication

Title: The peace : a warrior's journey / Roméo Dallaire.
Names: Dallaire, Roméo, author.
Description: Includes index.
Identifiers: Canadiana (print) 20230477208 | Canadiana (ebook) 20230477216 |
    ISBN 9780345814401 (hardcover) | ISBN 9780345814425 (EPUB)
Subjects: LCSH: Dallaire, Roméo. | LCSH: Peace. | LCSH: International relations. |
    LCSH: Security, International.
Classification: LCC JZ5538 .D35 2024 | DDC 327.1/72—dc23

Text and jacket design: Andrew Roberts
Jacket image: Hanna / Adobe Stock

Printed and bound in Canada

10 9 8 7 6 5 4 3 2 1

Penguin
Random House
RANDOM HOUSE CANADA

Pour Marie, qui m'a guidée comme Béatrice l'a fait pour Dante

CONTENTS

PART THREE: PEACE

INTRODUCTION

Midway upon the journey of our life,
I found myself within a forest dark.

Dante, *Inferno*, Canto i

H aving lived through biblical horror, and then a lifetime
since trying to fathom it, I share my path here in hopes
that it may help others whose absolute desire is lasting
peace. Including those, such as myself, who were trained
in war.

In April 1994, the lush and beautiful country of Rwanda—
where I had been tasked with a United Nations mission to
assist in the implemention of a peace accord where peace did
not exist—descended into genocide. Eight hundred thousand
dead in a hundred days. Millions mutilated, orphaned and displaced. Cycles of generational trauma set in motion. All a full
half century after the Holocaust, despite the world's relentless
refrain "never again."

Rwanda and its people, and my peacekeeping mission,
were abandoned to the killing. When I begged for help, I was
reminded that there was no oil in Rwanda, no diamonds,
nothing else of strategic importance. There were only human
beings—Black lives that didn't matter. For decades after the

mass slaughter ended, I was haunted by the spirits of the dead, the cries of the abandoned, the anguish of survivors, and the guilt of being powerless to stop the slaughter. And I struggled to find answers to impossible questions: *How? Why? What if?*

If I had not lived the experience of Rwanda, I would have carried on serving in the Canadian Armed Forces, eventually retiring as a general with three stars, a fishing rod and a plaque. I would have gone on to a civilian job and volunteer work, like so many of my colleagues trained in the Cold War era did. I suppose I could have forced myself along that predictable path when I got back from Rwanda—my family and my commanders clearly hoped I would get back to "normal"—but the genocide had completely shifted my perspective on who I was and what I stood for. It shocked me into a profound realization of the precious frailty of life and a deep consciousness of my relationship with the whole of humanity.

In other words, I found my soul. I came home injured, yes, and went on to suffer post-traumatic stress disorder (PTSD) and an even deeper moral injury of a scale and duration that several times brought me to the brink of suicide. But I was also imbued with a vision of our shared humanity and my own responsibility to it. This vision drove me to recognize that I had been going in the wrong direction—and not only me, but the military, the whole system. Rather than continuing to focus on winning wars, we needed to set our minds on shaping peace.

The Genocide against the Tutsi in Rwanda prompted a generation of scholars, politicians, soldiers, lawyers and humanitarians to seek new ways to prevent another such failure of humanity. We set up tribunals, crafted doctrine and produced countless reports on how to protect civilians from massive abuse, including genocide. But these efforts have not brought the peace we sought; instead, they've served as temporary and often superficial truces, briefly silencing guns and stabilizing frictions without resolving their fundamental causes.

Over the past thirty years, the genocide has been the driving force behind my relentless advocacy work on the prevention of mass atrocities and the protection of civilians, my efforts to end the use of children in armed conflict and the proliferation of nuclear weapons, and to help lift the taboos around operational stress injuries like the ones I suffered. I'd also been given the mandate to conduct a full reform of the officer corps, so that going forward no Canadian officer tasked with leading a UN peace mission would be as unprepared as I was for what they would encounter. I engaged in endless initiatives: the Will to Intervene guidance aimed at implementing the new Responsibility to Protect (R2P) doctrine; founding the Dallaire Institute for Children, Peace and Security, which drafted the Vancouver Principles on Peacekeeping and the Prevention of the Recruitment and Use of Child Soldiers; and partnering with the United Nations, the Government of Canada, Kofi Annan's genocide prevention advisory board, Wounded Warriors Canada, the Montreal Institute for Genocide and Human Rights Studies (MIGS), the Harvard Kennedy School, the Pugwash conferences, and the international Principles for Peace (P4P) commission to provide a covenant for lasting peace. My engagement in these efforts was directly linked to my guilt over witnessing mass murder on an unimaginable scale without being able to stop it.

My inner torment during those decades after the geno-cide is well documented. Coming from a military family and a career spent preparing for war, I worked with punishing zeal—lecturing, advising, writing, berating, all with the aim of uncovering a new understanding of peace. Long after the international community had put the incredible atrocities into the past, content to move on to the next crisis, I contin-ued to dedicate my days and nights to these efforts. Yet over and over, as various doctrines and initiatives were launched and fell short, I saw that we had still not cracked the code. Though humanity kept trying to get far enough ahead of catastrophes to prevent them, we kept failing.

Today, polarization, proxy wars, hybrid warfare that com-bines conventional tactics with online propaganda, geopoliti-cal tensions, large-scale violations of human rights, and the erosion of representative government all make peacebuilding increasingly complex. The recent impact of the COVID-19 pandemic, climate change and war on supply chains and food and energy prices highlights the interconnectedness and interdependence of a globalized world. Overall, we seem to be barely managing crises as they pop up, rather than acting to prevent such massive suffering. I still hope to be part of the wave of thought and activism that changes that.

I received my military training in the Cold War. At that time peace was viewed as a détente between the communist East and the capitalist West, reinforced by the mutually assured destruction of a balance of nuclear weapons between us. Like many others, I saw the end of the Cold War in 1989 as the opportunity to judiciously draw down armies and defence spending and focus on humanitarian efforts. And Europe, despite its long history of antagonism among nationals, did make strides in establishing and maintaining peace based on economic prosperity, human rights and a union of effort.

At the same time, however, three major powers—China, Russia and the United States—used the end of the Cold War to increase their military might. Russia has since become a giant rogue state, invading Ukraine in 2022 and attempting to gather allies wherever US influence has ebbed, namely in Syria, the Middle East and parts of Africa. China's true ambitions are still murky, but clearly reach beyond its current borders. Despite some isolationist moments, the US sees itself as the single entity that guarantees the security of the entire world, deploying its power throughout the globe. In stark contrast to the European doves, American hawks still see the exercise of power as the only way to peace.

So, decades after the Berlin Wall fell, we have stumbled back into a power-based world of alliances, where truces are more fragile now than they have been in decades. History continues to repeat ad nauseum. Peacekeepers by the tens of thousands are patrolling, observing and sporadically intervening in complex conflict zones, armed with limited resources and, too often, let down by outdated and superficial training, ambiguous mandates and inadequate leadership. Darfur, Mali, Congo, Afghanistan, Myanmar: in every case the world either turns its back entirely, as it did in Rwanda, or sends thoughts and prayers and guns. In some places, like Syria after the Arab Spring, the international community doesn't even really try to intervene, or else, as in Libya with the fall of Muammar Qaddafi, it makes the situation so very much worse.

Faced with the unpredictability of Vladimir Putin and his war against Ukraine (and the volatility of the Islamic State, al-Shabab, Hamas, populist white nationalists and all other malcontent extremists), we continually fall back on the same old tools and tactics. So much so that as I write these words, we find ourselves in another cold war, paralyzed into inaction by Russia's bluff over launching nuclear bombs. We met Putin's threats with sanctions and censure, and a lot of weapons and money for Ukraine (none of which, it should be noted, had been offered to Rwanda), but still we do not dare cross borders to protect the civilians whose country has been invaded, whose homes are being bombed, and who are being abused, displaced and killed.

The hard right everywhere is watching Putin with interest. To me, this era seems an awful lot like the 1930s: while a majority of middle powers are coming together with ideas for peaceful solutions, nationalists are increasing their power; there is no common ground between progressive ideas around peacebuilding and the "big power" concept of "securing" peace. This creates great uncertainty in the southern half of the world, where countries are not sure which power bloc to play ball with.

We had plenty of warning the invasion of Ukraine was coming—the *nearly ten years* since the Russians went into Crimea in 2014—and still we were unable to prevent the escalation. The "classic" tools and metrics used by the international community—the diplomatic exchanges, embargoes, self-interested assessments of resources (are there fuel, minerals and food reserves to protect or only unimportant human beings?), and aversion to casualties (to stay on the good side of media and voters)—none of it has changed. How can we be surprised when the results are the same? If we had really progressed in our united ambitions for peace, as soon as Russia edged its toes up to the border with Ukraine, NATO (the North Atlantic Treaty Organization) or the UN member states or both would have reinforced the line with boots on the ground. In our imperfect world today, the only way to struggle for peace is still with a show of willingness to fight.

Surely there has to be something more we can do. I have spent years reaching for that something more—a way to bring true and lasting peace. A revolutionary strategy for conflict prevention. A covenant of respect for the individual human being, instead of the nation-state. A shared understanding that engages all parties, from community groups to international bodies, from pulpits to command posts. An *ensemble* solution that reflects our increasingly borderless existence on this planet, where we are all equally vulnerable to climate change at the largest scale and to a virus at the smallest.

Conflicts that regenerate again and again after impotent peace agreements keep distracting us from coming together to face the greatest risks to our survival. If we cannot agree on a cohesive strategy to anticipate and mitigate conflicts among ourselves, how can we expect to resolve problems that will affect the whole of humanity?

———

Descending into hell in 1994 and then struggling up and out with only the vaguest glimmer of hope to guide me, I did learn many lessons. But I was too wounded and battle-scarred to see beyond the emotional and intellectual purgatory I remained mired in, until I found a way out of my own dark forest through loving and being loved. After I happily married in 2020, I could at last see with clarity the path I needed to take and the lodestars I needed to follow. To guide my thinking beyond the cycles I seemed to be stuck in, I turned—not for the first time—to the poets for inspiration.

Dante Alighieri (1265–1321) forged the way for an epoch that provides a profound example of the revolutionary human potential that can arise from a period of sustained peace: the Italian Renaissance. In that relatively short era came about a massive shift in fundamental thinking from theological to humanist. Dante's best known and most beloved work, *La Commedia* (so revered it was later renamed *The Divine Comedy*), completed the year before he died, is an epic poem in three parts that follows the poet as he travels through the Christian afterlife, starting in the desperate depths of *Inferno* (hell), up through the treacherous levels of *Purgatorio* (purgatory), and then, after he passes through a wall of fire, into *Paradiso* (heaven). And the journey does not end there. Instead, he continues up and up, learning more and better lessons until he reaches the pinnacle, an unknowable place beyond.

This poem almost literally conveys the arc of my own life's journey. Dante (as the poem's main character) found himself witnessing eternal torments divided into distinct and worsening circles of hell: limbo, lust, gluttony, wrath, heresy, violence, fraud, treachery. I, too, was an outsider who travelled through a genocidal hell that was sparked and sustained by human sins of omission and commission: deceit, disinterest, self-interest, ignorance, fear, othering, hate, revenge, denial. These are the failures that engender and sustain all wars.

Once Dante enters purgatory, the sinners he encounters are of a lesser order, but they are in constant danger of slipping back to hell if they indulge in any one of the seven deadly sins. In similar fashion, humanity's current best efforts to prevent war and aim for peace are undone by stagnant cycles of truce, devotion to the status quo, self-interest, disorder, ethical failures, irresponsibility, and inequality. In the poem (as for us today), the suffering in purgatory is tamed ever so slightly by awareness and growth, and therein lies the hope.

I immediately recognized my own late metamorphosis in the image of the terrifying wall of fire Dante must pass through to reach paradise. A few years ago, I went through a similar crisis of transformation after I was faced with the consequences of the path of self-destruction I'd been travelling for twenty-five years, racing around the world, juggling pro bono efforts on behalf of child soldiers, injured veterans and victims of mass atrocities, living out of suitcases and eating fast food in airports, always alone, always on high alert, devoid of any inner solace, haunted always by the uneasy spirits of the genocide's victims that invaded my dreams and waking thoughts. Despite my relentlessness, I *still* wasn't finding solutions for lasting peace in the world, and the doctors told me if I kept on that way, I would die. And soon.

At that moment of extreme vulnerability, a new dimension of life entered my closed-off world: I fell in love, and through this solace and safe harbour, I gained a new lease and a new perspective on life.

Today I feel I am travelling a path to peace that has previously eluded me. In Part Three of this book, I'll share the lodestars I'm following now, in hopes that they might be of some help to others in leaping through that wall of fire and finding unity with each other and our planet. It won't be fast, and it won't be easy, but I am living proof that it is possible to achieve such transformational change.

Humanity's problems are increasingly borderless. Too many of us react to this reality by putting up walls that allow us (we think) to protect ourselves and forget about others. But putting one's faith in state power, nationalism and the use of force to keep us "safe" behind our home borders is a bet that won't be won. Such narrow thinking is no longer possible in our interconnected world. We need strategic local and global leadership to actively predict and prevent problems before they turn into catastrophes. Only in this way can we prevent suffering and insecurity and look toward a state I call The Peace.

Of course, I understand that for some there is comfort and even satisfaction in staying true to the status quo. But such a purgatory is not peace. It is merely truce, continuously vulnerable to frictions that have never been addressed, use of force and abuse of power, and the constant overarching threat of annihilation posed by nuclear weapons and climate change.

As Dante hesitates before entering paradise, afraid for himself and afraid of the unknown, his guide smiles at him and shakes his head, asking, "Now, really, do you want to stay back there?"

I know I don't, and I believe today's younger generations are similarly impatient with the band-aid solutions and divisive inequality of the past. I believe these generations without borders will readily leap through the fire to embrace an entirely new perspective on the human condition.

For the sure and brave, I offer this book as my humble effort to lay out the issues as I've witnessed them and to provide some inspiration that may help guide your way. I can't wait to see where you lead.

Peux que ce veux. Allons-y! Where there's a will, there's a way. Let's go!

Roméo Dallaire, January 11, 2023

PART ONE

HELL

I here descended to the nether Hell

                              Dante, *Inferno*, Canto XII

n the spring of 1994, the tiny African nation of Rwanda
ignited into a living inferno. Hundreds of thousands of
children, men and women slaughtered. Millions maimed
and left to rot. Babies hacked from their mother's wombs.
Elders gasping their last breaths in muddy ditches. Girls split
in two. Rivers running red with blood. This was not war as I
had been trained to fight it. This was hell on Earth.

The scenes I witnessed in Rwanda were burned in my
psyche and still send up flares thirty years later. But many
have forgotten what unfolded in that country. Many never
knew. Some who are reading this now were not even born.
For them—for you—I will provide a very brief review.
Because I want you to remember. I want you to know. And
most importantly, I want you to understand the catastrophic
and potentially avoidable failures that led to and prevailed

through and out the other side of this genocide, so that you recognize them when you see them again. Recognize them as the sources and signs of *all* mass atrocities and wars, in hopes they can be avoided, even actively prevented, from happening in the future. Because Rwanda is just one nightmarish example of the many conflicts in volatile states that devolve into unconscionable human suffering. Hell on Earth didn't appear for the first time in Rwanda, and it still exists, consuming lives and thwarting our ambitions for a peaceful world.

The last hundred years has been called the Century of Genocides. Few regions in the world remain unaffected by mass slaughter aimed at eliminating a particular ethnic or political group: 35 million Chinese, 10.5 million Slavs, 6 million Jewish Europeans, 3 million Cambodians, 1.6 million Tibetans, 1.5 million Bengalis, 1.5 million Armenians, 1 million Vietnamese, 500,000 Indonesians, 8,000 Muslim Bosnians, and countless people indigenous to the Americas.

While the numbers throughout Africa are similarly horrifying—genocidal slaughter of the Amhara and Agew in Ethiopia; the Nuer, Nuba and Dinka in South Sudan; Isaaqs in Somaliland; the Gukurahundi in Zimbabwe; the Darfuri in Sudan; the Igbo in Nigeria; the Herero and Nama in Namibia; and of course the Tutsi in Rwanda—the concept of mass human destruction was brought to Africa by white Europeans during the ruthless brutality of colonization (a tidy academic word that stands for the enslavement, plunder, rape, oppression, humiliation and murder of whichever Indigenous populations the French, British, Belgian, Prussian, Spanish, Dutch, Portuguese and other criminal pillagers chose to desecrate for their own gain).

Too often I have heard people from those colonizing nations describe Africa as "prone to violence," even insisting that the conflicts that erupted around the continent after the colonial overlords cut and ran in the 1960s were "tribal" in origin. That somehow those colonial overlords had kept a lid on such violence, when in fact it was the abuses and atrocities inflicted on the continent during and beyond the colonial era that prepared the ground for such horrors as the Genocide against the Tutsis in Rwanda.

The mass slaughter of specific groups of human beings, their treatment as less than vermin, without rights and without protection, is not a new or recent concept, nor does it have its origins in Africa. Much as we are taught otherwise, the concept and application of systematic, dehumanizing mass slaughter was developed and modelled by wealthy states: powerful imperial dynasties that permitted and even thrived on an overwhelming abuse of power.* History is replete with examples of powerful nations eliminating people

---

* As I will explore more thoroughly in Part Three, our current lexicon is missing some key terms to describe new ideas and changing perspectives. Making distinctions between countries with terms like "Third World" vs. "First World" or "developed" vs. "developing" is hierarchical and presumptive, assuming there is a superior state toward which all are striving. "Global West" vs. "Global South" is inaccurate (what about Japan? Cuba? Australia?). "Wealthy" vs. "poor" are fine if clearly speaking about GDP, but not as euphemisms: many resource-rich countries have low GDPs and many impoverished people live in wealthy nations. I will make every effort to name groups of nations descriptively instead ("industrialized," "sub-Saharan," "Indigenous," "European," "North American"). This tactic may be cumbersome in terms of syllables, but I hope is more accurate and less offensive.

whose only crime was living their lives peacefully on land the colonizer took a mild interest in, be it the Belgians in Congo, the British in India, the Spanish, French, and British in the Indigenous lands of North America, the Americans in what became the United States, the French in Madagascar, the Portuguese in Angola, the Italians in Ethiopia, the Japanese in China, the Spanish in Mexico, the Germans in Namibia, and on and on.

Back to the nightmarish example I know best. Before European colonization, the Great Lakes region of Africa was home to multiple kingdoms. The lush hills around Lake Kivu were populated mainly by the Hutu people, who farmed the land, and by a smaller group, called the Tutsi, who primarily herded cattle. Since keeping cattle generated slightly more wealth than farming, over hundreds of years economic differences developed between these two originally quite similar groups.

When the Belgians began their brutal colonial rule over Rwanda, they decreed that the Hutu and the Tutsi were *ethnically* different, dehumanizing both groups by measuring and categorizing them in arbitrary, Eurocentric ways. The Belgians imposed identity cards on all and showed preferential treatment to the Tutsi (who were considered to be slightly taller and lighter skinned, so more European-looking, than the Hutu), exacerbating the small differences between the groups into inequalities and stoking long-standing resentments.

After Rwanda gained its independence from Belgium in 1962, the Hutu majority rose up against the Tutsi "elite," igniting decades of conflict between the groups. Many Tutsis fled to neighbouring countries: Uganda, Burundi and what is now the Democratic Republic of Congo. In 1990, Tutsi refugees who'd spent decades in Uganda returned to their homeland in force and established a stronghold in the north of Rwanda, displacing 600,000 Hutus.

After months of negotiations, in July 1993 the Hutu-dominated Rwandan government and the Tutsi-led Rwandan Patriotic Front (RPF) agreed, under enormous pressure from outside powers, to the possibility of a peace agreement at a meeting in Arusha, Tanzania. The Arusha Accords, as the agreement became known, were intended to end the long-standing civil war and create a power-sharing arrangement that would guarantee security to both the Tutsi and the Hutu. The accords would have ended Hutu-dominated rule in Rwanda by allocating seats to opposition parties and the Tutsi-dominated RPF in an interim transitional government that had a mandate to hold democratic elections within two years. Everyone also agreed that the accords would be implemented, monitored and supported by the United Nations Assistance Mission for Rwanda (UNAMIR). I was selected as that mission's force commander.

As I worked in good faith with both sides on the implementation of the accords, I began to realize that all was not as it seemed. I learned that weapons were being stockpiled in various locations, including the Hutu president's own home village. I was told that vast numbers of machetes were being imported, beyond the numbers needed to harvest crops and keep the thick jungle at bay. Schools were segregating children in classrooms according to the ethnicity listed on their government-issued identity cards (Tutsi on one side, Hutu on the other). The youth political group called the Interahamwe, which was linked to the hardline Hutu party, was increasingly belligerent, with rumours of members being trained as a militia in the Great Forest in the southwestern part of the country. Though my mission was not provided with a Kinyarwandan translator (a mystifying decision), we were still able to note a worrying tone building in the broadcasts from the extremist Hutu-run radio station, RTLM. After receiving confirmation from a reliable informant of an extremist Hutu plan to "exterminate" the Tutsi, on January 11, 1994, I sent what has since been called the "Genocide fax" to my commanders at the United Nations. I wrote, "It is our intention to take action within the next 36 hours"—first reconnoitring and then raiding the arms cache and confiscating the weapons we'd learned the extremists were intending to use.

I understood my mission's objective was to implement an agreed-upon peace, an aim that I felt fully justified such a raid. The UN replied with a different objective: "the overriding consideration is the need to avoid entering into a course of action that might lead to the use of force." I was told to stand down under the rules of engagement of the Chapter VI mission I was commanding, where the use of force was allowed only in situations of self-defence.

Over the following three months I continued to work with the Tutsi RPF and the Hutu government forces to implement the peace accords, all the while arguing vehemently with the UN's Department of Peacekeeping Operations (DPKO) that the actions I wanted to take in regard to the arms caches were essential to disrupt the extremist planning. I never stopped insisting to my bosses at the UN that the political stalemate among the parties and the clear escalation of subversive actions (assassinations, riots, attacks on moderates) signalled a potentially catastrophic situation that I did not have the resources (troops, ammunition, weapons) to address.

My constant haranguing finally convinced them. A couple of weeks before the start of the genocide, I received approval to conduct these operations. It was too late. We had lost the opportunity to disrupt preparations for the subsequent slaughter.

On April 6, 1994, the Rwandan president's plane was shot down. By whom, we still aren't sure—a full, independent investigation has never been conducted. But the effect was like a secret starter pistol had gone off. The mass killing began.

Thousands of Tutsi (as well as moderate Hutu) civilians were specifically targeted and brutally murdered by their extremist Hutu neighbours in the days that immediately followed. By the end of the first twenty-four hours, ten Belgian peacekeepers under my command had been disarmed and beaten to death by enraged anti-Belgian government soldiers and veterans. The Hutu extremists had clearly noticed how fast the United States had pulled out of Mogadishu, Somalia, after eighteen US soldiers were killed there six months earlier. Arranging for the targeting of Belgian soldiers, when they could have picked from any of my field troops, all of whom were in vulnerable positions, was carefully calculated to cause just enough diplomatic, political and media panic in the nations that were contributing troops for them to withdraw their forces, but not enough to motivate a rein-forcement of my UN mission.

And it worked: Belgium, as well as France, Italy, the United States and others immediately sent trucks and planes to evac-uate their troops and expats, abandoning the mission as well as the Rwandan people. Over 2,000 UNAMIR peacekeepers were withdrawn by their nations. As they left, Canada sent me a dozen staff officers to help rebuild my HQ, though I had requested a battalion of 800. My mission was reduced to about 450 peacekeepers—mostly from Ghana and Tunisia, a few from Senegal and Poland, and a scattering of others—all of whom bravely agreed to stay.

The UN could not persuade the international community to provide reinforcements, resources or even political capital to the mission. And so, two weeks into what we in the field had already identified as a genocide, Boutros Boutros-Ghali, the secretary-general of the United Nations, personally called to order me and my remaining troops to withdraw for fear of further UN casualties. I refused. I could not abandon these people. If there was little we could do to help, we would at the very least bear witness.

So our small remaining force stayed on through the grow-ing slaughter, with no resources, no mission statement and no authority to protect the tens of thousands of civilians flock-ing to our five remaining posts in the capital city of Kigali. Five more of my peacekeepers were killed in action in the weeks that followed. Tens of thousands of civilian Rwandans were slaughtered every day that passed. We did not sleep, we did not eat; when our drinking water ran out, we drank the green dew that pooled on the roof outside of my office. The extremist Hutu radio station, RTLM, blared instructions on how to wield a machete to inflict the most damage with the least effort, how to lop off extremities (hands, feet, genitals) so the victim would bleed to death slowly rather than all at once. Tutsis were ushered into churches by their neighbours, under the ruse of protection, only to have the doors barricaded and every one of them slaughtered.

Over the following three months, as a thousand individuals were being hacked to pieces every hour, and rats grew to the size of dogs from feasting on the bodies in the streets, we managed to protect around thirty thousand Rwandans who had been able to reach the five protection sites we had established almost entirely on the bluff of our blue berets.

I sent daily reports to the UN, demanding reinforcements. I pleaded with every foreign journalist I could find, imploring them to tell the world what was happening. My mission became one of fielding demands from the UN and its member countries to evacuate remaining expatriates, negotiating ceasefires and truces, and constantly arguing for the cessation of hostilities and an end to the wanton killing. I waited in vain for help to arrive. No one wanted to get involved in trying to stop the slaughter, and many trivialized the situation as predictable African "tribalism."

On July 4, Kigali fell to the Tutsi RPF. By July 18 the RPF had established an interim, predominantly Tutsi government. By August, the slaughter was over. The RPF had defeated the extremist government forces and chased the Hutu *génocid-aires* out of the country.

I shared the facts of my mission in my first book, *Shake Hands with the Devil*. I showed its impact on my work in my second book, *They Fight Like Soldiers, They Die Like Children*. I revealed its effect on my life in *Waiting for First Light*, the memoir I wrote about my struggle with PTSD. I do not intend to retell those stories here. But in the following pages I will again delve into the example of Rwanda, because I was there. As commander of the UN forces, I was actively, desperately trying to negotiate peace before, during and after a three-month-long genocide that left 800,000 dead, countless injured, and four million displaced and forced to flee. It was a time that epitomized hell on Earth for me and everyone who lived it. And it followed the relentless pattern—from deceit at its outset to denial long after the killings ceased—that is always present in these explosions of violence, a pattern that traps us in an endless cycle of conflict to this day. Rwanda has become my lens.

Major Philip Lancaster served with me in Rwanda. Like me, he sustained severe operational stress injuries there. With a PhD in philosophy, Phil has helped me to apply Plato's allegory of the cave as a way to understand the unfolding of the genocide as I experienced it.

Plato asks us to imagine prisoners chained in a cave so that all they can see of the outside world are the shadows of people, as they pass by a fire, reflected on the cave walls. With little to do to pass the time, the prisoners talk among themselves and speculate about what the shadows might mean.

Though none of them can know the truth of these passersby, arguments break out as each tries to create a coherent story from shadow and imagination.

This is a disturbingly apt description of what it felt like to be a United Nations peacekeeper plunged into the middle of Rwanda as tensions built toward the outbreak of the genocide. We could not see what was really happening around us. All we could see were fragments of shadows, never the complete picture.

Unlike Plato's cave dwellers, we had many more sources of information that could be checked against each other. We kept records and were able to move about to talk to people. But we could never completely uncover the truth because some of the shadows shown to us were deliberately false, while we built others from the fabric of our own illusions.

With reflection, research and the passage of time, I have made some progress in finding my way out of that cave. My goal with this part of this book is to use those hard-won insights to uncover the infernal, rudimentary and ideally *preventable* failures at the root of all wars and mass atrocities. If we can see them clearly, we can reject them for the toxic lies and evasions they truly are.

To paraphrase *The Divine Comedy*, you have to go down to go up.

DECEIT

Many of the Devil's vices . . . among them,
That he's a liar and the father of lies.

Dante, *Inferno*, Canto XXIII

D eceit has always been a means of survival. Think of a Stone Age hunter using branches as camouflage, or a bird faking a broken wing to lure a predator away from its young. In the military, deception is often crucial to operations. I am not naive about this. The principles of war condone the intentional deception of the enemy for tactical advantage—for instance, the use of subterfuge in intelligence gathering or to achieve the element of surprise. Both sides in a battle, and the commanders of the war the battle is part of, expect such tactics.

However, after thirty years of thinking about the lingering questions raised by the Genocide in Rwanda, I've grown to understand that the secrets and lies I was subjected to during my mission were deeper and more convoluted than those I'd been trained to expect. Had I been duped from the start? Could it be that I not only failed to solve the problems, but exacerbated them, even so far as to unwittingly assist the extremists? Were we—me, the UN, our political masters—all set up to fail?

With the benefit of hindsight, I can now see that one of our key mistakes going into Rwanda was that we in what I'll call the West (for lack of a better catch-all) were all too eager to impose a simple, moderate solution of power-sharing and democracy on this conflict. Because of our biases about how the world "should" work, we deceived ourselves into thinking the moderate leaders in Rwanda would find a way to a compromise and that the hardliners would follow. I know that I, for one, truly believed all parties to the accords had peace as their ambition (at least, their perception of peace).

What I and others failed to see was that behind the key figures sitting around the negotiating tables in Arusha was a set of people with extremist views locked into what they believed was an existential conflict they couldn't afford to lose. We thought we were dealing with disagreements that could be overcome through dialogue, trust building and compromise, failing completely to understand the chasm that separated the parties from each other and from us. Western nations had imposed differences on Rwandans for generations, and now here they were, imposing solutions.

But now I also wonder how much our naive optimism was encouraged deliberately by people and agencies with their own agendas. I say "our" because, as force commander, I was part of a much larger diplomatic and humanitarian effort, led by good people who wanted a peaceful solution and believed it would be possible. Were we all fooled? Was UNAMIR a real attempt at peace or a token effort providing cover for the self-interest of certain nation-state members of the Security Council?

The Belgians, French and Americans all publicly supported the peace accords, but then they failed to provide the resources the peacekeeping mission required. Similarly suspicious, in the final weeks of the peace negotiations, the Americans imposed an ultimatum on the parties at the table: find agreement or lose US support. Did they understand that this new pressure to come to an immediate consensus was gasoline on a spark? Such an unreasonable timeline had never been forced onto the parties in conflict in Northern Ireland, say, or in Israel. Was this pressure an error in judgment on the part of the Americans or a deliberate strategy aimed at blowing up the process? It certainly undermined the potential for a peaceful and successful implementation of the accords.

The United Nations itself occupies an awkward space between the expectations it raises and its capacity to deliver. Some expect it to act as a world government and some as the world's army or police force. But the UN is made up of 193 member states. Those nations provide the funds and the troops for any intervention; the UN has no authority or ability to act independently. From the outside, the UN may look like a stable institution dedicated to furthering worthy causes—such as world peace—but its member states hold distinct, often antithetical, values. Going in, I suspected the UN might be as dysfunctional as any large organization run by collective input from disparate actors, but I was shocked to experience deceptive behaviour not only from its member nations, but even among the specialized agencies of the UN itself.

Major Brent Beardsley, my executive assistant on the mission, was the one and only Canadian officer my government originally provided to deploy with me, instead of the battalion of infantry I had requested. He came with me to UN headquarters in New York in 1993 to begin building our mission from scratch. Neither of us had any knowledge of Rwanda, nor even of sub-Saharan Africa. The only Great Lakes we knew were the ones between Canada and the US.

Before the internet, it was much harder to accumulate the kind of knowledge and insight we needed, because it was contained within the silos of academic departments, think tanks, non-governmental organizations (NGOs) and UN agencies. Each discipline, each organization, had its own vocabulary designed to enable deep discussion among its closed circles of experts, but not necessarily between those experts and the uninitiated. I have since discovered that there were sources of insight I could have tapped to pierce the layers of agendas and lies all around us, but at the time I simply had no hope of finding them; my education, like that of most career military officers, had not given me a broad enough set of tools to know where to look.

The internet can lead you to good information and experts willing to share what they know, but it is itself a tool of deception, containing so many conflicting sources that it requires exceptional research skills to sort the good from the bad. Anyway, that was not an option in 1993. Brent and I hoped, if we looked hard enough, that we would be able to locate some repository of top-secret documentation to guide our mission, but we discovered that no diplomat nor UN official seemed fully knowledgeable when it came to the small, non-strategic country of Rwanda. Or if they were, they were unwilling to share.

I experienced this kind of information hoarding again ten years later, when Kofi Annan (secretary-general of the UN at the time) invited me, Archbishop Desmond Tutu, Gareth Evans, and four others to join his advisory board on genocide prevention. From the start, we were thwarted in our noble (but I believed achievable) goal because we couldn't secure permission and agreement even inside the UN to collate information from its various agencies to conduct our analyses. We tried to gather diverse data, given that everything from demographics to economics to historical frictions exacerbated by the imposition of colonial boundaries could prove useful in signalling the potential for a situation to turn catastrophic. But we were unsuccessful. Some deceptions are far more malevolent, but the devious stonewalling within the UN struck me as unnecessary and unbecoming of the institution.

While we prepared for the mission, for instance, we did not know that the French and Belgians were still supporting the Hutu government's army, the Rwandan Government Forces (RGF), with training and weapons under a long-standing military co-operation agreement, despite a string of documented massacres committed by the troops they had trained and supplied.

In fact, in addition to France and Belgium, the UK and the US also had military attachés in place in their embassies in the capitals of Uganda and Rwanda, respectively. Each of those governments must have had detailed intelligence they failed to share with me, despite their "commitment" to the mission. They had to have some knowledge of the mobilization and training of hardline Hutu militias, yet they kept silent. As did all the other delegations, including those from neighbouring African countries, who also must have had some idea. Was this merely to avoid committing real resources to a mission they had no sincere interest in, or was it a calculated attempt by some to hold onto influence in the region by supporting one of the antagonists?

Journalists and historians have since detailed France's machinations to maintain influence in the region through their support of President Juvénal Habyarimana's twenty-year-long Hutu-dominated regime. Those efforts were officially confirmed in a 2021 report commissioned by the French government, which prompted President Emmanuel Macron to ask for "the gift of forgiveness" from the people of Rwanda for France's "heavy and damning responsibilities" in the genocide.

Habyarimana had signed a military co-operation agreement with France shortly after assuming power in 1973 and had called on French military support to halt the first Tutsi RPF invasion in 1990, and RPF attacks in 1992 and 1993. Indeed, both the French and the Belgians had conducted military training and support missions to the government forces in the years leading up to my deployment; until mid-December 1993, there was still a small French infantry battalion stationed in Kigali.

Even once I was on the ground in Rwanda, the French continued to argue that UNAMIR was nothing but a show being put on by the UN. The French ambassador, his military attaché and the head of the French gendarmerie all insisted to me that five hundred military observers could easily achieve the aim of assisting the peace process.

At the time I thought their lack of support for the mission came from a genuine hope that some kind of compromise would work. But now I know that behind the scenes, the Mitterrand government was manoeuvring with Habyarimana and Hutu extremists in the RGF to undermine our force's effectiveness. I do not think the French had any idea that a full-scale genocide was looming. However, they definitely had to have been expecting retaliations between the antagonists, and even mass atrocities. I am sure they believed the risk of such bloodshed was worth it if it kept Rwanda as an unofficial neo-colony of France. These deceptions and sins of omission made my mission less effective; worse, I now believe the people I met during the weeks before I deployed likely saw my lack of knowledge as a factor to be taken advantage of.

And from the point of view of the diplomats and military attachés, why not? Structural deception is built into the fabric of international diplomacy: what is agreed to in public isn't always what goes on behind the scenes.

We see this today in the gap separating commitments made at UN meetings about climate change and what nations deliver after all the speeches and galas are over. We also see it with the Convention on the Rights of the Child, which has been ratified by every country on Earth—with the sole exception of the United States—and its Optional Protocol on child soldiers, as well as the more recent Vancouver Principles to prevent the recruitment and use of child soldiers, now endorsed by more than 105 countries. Despite these agreements to protect them, children continue to be recruited into violent conflict by the thousands.

As Brent and I conducted our initial mission assessment, we may not have known what we did not know, but we did feel as though everyone around us was in on some secret arrangement to find excuses, dispute evidence and turn a blind eye when necessary to avoid spending money or taking risks. Since Brent and I took the UN Charter principles as a given, this seemed bizarre to us.

It is true that the UN's Department of Peacekeeping Operations, then run by Kofi Annan and a Canadian I respected and knew well, General Maurice Baril, was overwhelmed by the massive increase of deployments to conflict zones arising out of the end of the Cold War. And that the relatively benign Chapter VI peacekeeping mission, where the last thing a Blue Beret was meant to do was *fight* to protect the peace, was not proving effective in places where there was no real peace to keep. The world was entering into a whole new phase of imploding nations, failed states and mass atrocities on a scale never imagined, with little to no effective command and control capabilities in the New York headquarters.

Still, we needed to figure out who was playing what games in and around Rwanda. The Habyarimana government, for example, had been sending diplomats to the UN for years. In 1993 and 1994, it even had a seat on the UN Security Council, where it was well placed to influence or delay decisions, particularly given unqualified support from France, one of the council's five permanent members (the P5). It is incredible to picture Rwanda's representative sitting in the UN chambers debating peace while the country was prepping for war. Given this privileged insider observation post, Rwandan government hardliners had plenty of information at their disposal to predict what would happen—or rather what would *not* happen—if they followed an extremist path.

At the time, France's African policy was run directly from President François Mitterrand's office. While members of this policy group, calling itself the African Cell and directed by the president's son, styled themselves as champions of enlightened democratic politics, they deceptively fostered and maintained a close personal relationship with President Habyarimana. As a result, his Hutu Power extremist party received unstinting support from Mitterrand and his accomplices, without the French parliament or the public ever knowing. They attempted to cloak their nefarious actions in support of a genocidal regime by misrepresenting Operation Turquoise (their UN-mandated military presence in Rwanda at the ebbing of the genocide) as a neutral humanitarian protection force. When I worked with the representatives of the African Cell, the French Foreign Office and the French Defence Department on the ground, I clearly saw that—while all three had unique perspectives on what to do in Rwanda—they were all supporting the Hutu extremist government. Research conducted after the genocide to piece together the chain of cause and effect that led to it points to a multi-layered deception going on in the 1990s within the Rwandan government. Arusha Accords or not, Habyarimana and his party were desperate to hang onto power. He was also under severe economic pressure because of a drastic drop in the price of coffee and tin, Rwanda's major sources of revenue, aside from foreign aid. And aid donors were getting impatient with the ongoing mistreatment of Tutsis. The competition for a declining share of state revenues, plus relentless population growth and a massive drought in the late 1980s that undermined the country's food security, saw all Rwandans suffer. Finally, there was growing military pressure on the Habyarimana government from the Tutsi-led RPF, who, after they'd invaded, had hunkered down inside the country's northern borders as the Arusha process ground on.

In 1990, President Habyarimana had duplicitously announced that he supported the emergence of ten different minor opposition parties in Rwanda; his intention was in fact to fracture his opposition while delaying the move toward multi-party democracy. As he was struggling to survive by saying one thing in public and doing something else behind the scenes, Habyarimana's wife was busy running a shadow cabinet, known in French as *le Clan de Madame* or in Kinyarwanda as the *akazu*, which consisted mostly of northerners from her own clan. From *le Clan de Madame* hatched *Réseau zéro* (the Zero Network), a clandestine subgroup dedicated to the "liquidation" of Tutsis and moderate Hutus in hopes of preserving a stranglehold on the Rwandan state.

While full and reliable accounts of the existence and impact of these elements can now be easily found, none of this was clear to me at the time. Indications of what was being planned began to emerge in January 1994, but even then, it looked like a chance still existed that the six-month old peace agreement could be saved with bold action against those who were threatening it.

As I pointed out in *Shake Hands with the Devil*, the Ugandan government was also playing games of deception. Along with UNAMIR, I'd been asked to lead the United Nations Observer Mission Uganda-Rwanda (UNOMUR), a mission designed to monitor the border between the two countries and shut off Ugandan military support to the RPF. Uganda said it supported the UN's aims at the same time as its army blocked us on the ground. A large Tutsi refugee population had lived in the south of Uganda, close to the Rwandan border, since they'd been forced into exile in the late 1950s. Because of tensions inside Uganda over the long stay of those refugees, President Yoweri Museveni had pushed the Tutsi RPF to go back to Rwanda, but he also wanted to continue to support them. (At the time, it was difficult to grasp how well developed the RPF and the Ugandan political and senior military cultures were, and how closely some factions within them were linked.)

The RPF members themselves were desperate to find their way back to Rwanda; even though they dominated the population of southern Uganda, their refugee status kept them outsiders within their host country. In a much later very candid conversation, Paul Kagame, who was then the leader of the RPF and now is the president of Rwanda, confided to me that during his many years in the Ugandan military, he was blocked from the highest ranks because he was Tutsi, even though he had been instrumental in supporting Museveni and getting rid of the former Ugandan president, Idi Amin. There may have been some remaining loyalty at work in Museveni's continuing support of the RPF, but there was also the fact that he needed the RPF to be successful: Uganda did *not* want the Tutsis back.

Meanwhile, France was also lying about its support of the border-monitoring mission, saying yes to UNOMUR in public and then quietly undermining our efforts on the ground. While France had supported a UN arms embargo to Rwanda, it had been supplying weapons and ammunition to the Hutu-led Rwandan government for decades and continued to do so. French government hardliners merely rerouted such deliveries through intermediaries.

It would be hard to find a better example of fellow travellers finding the same road convenient for different reasons.

This leads me to perhaps the biggest and most painful deception of all, the false promise of protection that UNAMIR offered to the Rwandan people. UNAMIR's Chapter VI mandate leading up to that fateful night in April expressly forbade us from actively protecting civilians, and as such would not provide us the troops, weapons and ammunition we would have needed to do so. UN insiders, the Rwandan government and the international member states may have found our Chapter VI mandate acceptable and clear, but its implications were far from obvious to the people most affected.

Even today, some people ask why I didn't simply race out into the streets to neutralize the belligerents. I wish they understood, after all these decades of me trying to explain, I was not provided with any offensive capabilities. A Chapter VI mission does not require them. We were equipped with a few rifles and pistols, no automatic weapons, and a few rounds of ammunition, and were easily overwhelmed by thousands upon thousands of *génocidaires* and Hutu government forces. Had I shot up the first ones I saw, they would have seen the entire UN mission as combat enemies and returned fire, and then gone on with their killing. My personal goal was to protect the people I could for as long as possible and continue to negotiate for ceasefire and peace, as all the while, I continued to plead with nations, media and the UN to reframe UNAMIR as a Chapter VII mission that would allow member states to provide me the troops, supplies and weapons we so desperately needed.

I will never forget the cries of the more than thirty thousand women, children and men who made it successfully through the killing barriers once the genocide began and flocked to UN sites for protection. We kept these relative few safe entirely by bluff. No matter what was written in the mandate, the Rwandan people saw the UN as a force that would protect them from the violence. And shame on all the countries of the world that make up the UN for not living up to that reasonable expectation.

The peace agreement was requested by moderates in both parties but dissenting extremists existed on both sides, and they used force and intimidation to prevent the moderates from openly expressing themselves in the negotiations. The peace process was designed to keep me and my UN forces distracted: the moderate parties at the table were either uninformed or bullied into silence by extremists (including the president's wife); the extremists kept working behind the scenes, knowing my mission was not permitted—and, more relevant, was not equipped—to intervene in what they were doing.

Given the circumstances, and the lack of funds, troops and political will to support UNAMIR, it was impossible to implement the peace accords. Both sides knew this. And the French, Belgian, American and British delegations to the UN in New York were all aware of the immense challenges, but they didn't say a word to me, the force commander attempting to do the job he thought he'd been given.

This might be too strong an accusation, yet I have a hard time believing that the Genocide in Rwanda unfolded because of innocent mistakes. What I can say with confidence is that, from the beginning, the UN as an institution didn't have much faith in the peace agreement; however, Rwandan and French political and military staff pushed Secretary-General Boutros-Ghali and the Security Council for a mission with a limited mandate that could be done on the cheap (the United States was not paying its dues, so money was scarce). If it worked, the Rwandans would have an agreement, the French could wash their hands of another endless African conflict, and the UN could gain a much-needed easy "win."

But this complex, volatile situation required so much more than anyone was willing to give. UNAMIR was a false front, a cardboard tank. And I, a paper tiger.

DISINTEREST

It careth not for its own proper flesh?

Dante, *Purgatorio*, Canto xx

In the first days of the genocide, a number of nations sent reconnaissance parties to assess the situation. At the debriefings, one told me, "General, we're going to recommend that no one get involved in this complicated mess. It may only be tribal and it may not last too long." Another said, "You know, there's nothing here for us. No strategic resources. The only thing here is people, and there are too many of them anyway."

It was not until six weeks later, with half a million massacred bodies strewn across the world's TV screens, that the UN Security Council finally agreed to call this "complicated mess" a genocide and approved a five-thousand troop reinforcement. I needed those troops, adequately trained and well supplied, as soon as I could get them, and only the big and middle powers could make that happen. They didn't. No one came until the killing stopped. The genocide was over in July. The first troops hit the ground in August. They were from Ethiopia, where a civil war had just ended; they arrived with no background in how to handle a peace agreement within the context of a UN structure. They didn't have ammunition. Or radios. Or supplies. It was too late, anyway.

Why did no one come to Rwanda? Because there was "nothing there." In my many dark moments, I have raged that if Rwanda's 350 mountain gorillas had been at risk, I would have received more support from the international community than I had with a million human lives on the line. Instead, I heard versions of this comment, over and over: "We just need to step back and let them slaughter each other for a few weeks, and then go in and pick up the pieces." François Mitterrand himself had been quoted by *Le Figaro* newspaper in 1988 as saying, "In countries like that, genocide is not too important."

I also heard over and over that member nations were loath to send troops because the recent deaths of the US soldiers in Mogadishu had destroyed the public's faith and interest in peacekeeping. Yet, between 1992 and 1996, the international community sent tens of thousands of peacekeeping troops into Yugoslavia. At the same time as the Genocide in Rwanda built up and then unfolded, unchecked, these nations were willing to step in to try to prevent "ethnic cleansing" in the former Yugoslavia. In fact, more people were raped, killed and displaced in Rwanda in *three months* than during four years of war in Bosnia. The clear message: to the international "community," Black Africans were less important, less precious, less deserving of assistance and sacrifice than other human beings. This was both disinterest and hypocrisy writ large. Of course, it shouldn't have been so surprising to me; during the colonial era, native populations and entire ethnic groups were wiped out by European nations at the same time as those nations were supporting human rights reforms at home.

The world had decided which people count and which don't. That grotesque pecking order of humanity, laid bare during the 1990s, still operates today. And it seems to me as vicious in intent and impact as it ever was in the colonial era.

While the causes of most African conflicts run deep and are difficult to tease apart—though responsibility rests heavily on the colonial powers—the roots of disinterest in helping to end those conflicts are relatively simple to name: politics and racism. The politics of self-interest keep certain countries, conflicts and people included in world policies and media. Racism keeps Africa *out*.

I tried for years to understand why it took so long, until it was far too late to intervene, for anyone outside Rwanda to believe that a genocide was happening. That the international community and the international media were largely indifferent to the monumental level of violence we were witnessing shocked me to my core. I suppose I had an exaggerated notion of the power of international public opinion to restrain bad actors. And an underappreciation of the international community's readiness to accept mass atrocities as a "normal" part of African politics.

Of course, the initial stages of the genocide were hidden by the general chaos on the ground, and at first every newsroom, embassy and government was overwhelmed with conflicting and confusing reports. But the speed with which French and Belgian paratroopers arrived to evacuate expatriates suggests that they had been ready for some kind of explosion and had contingency plans in place well in advance. Such planning springs from anticipation that reflects deep racial prejudice and, I dare say, cowardice, at least in the sense of being more concerned with saving one's own skin than doing the right thing. They took the warning signs seriously enough to save their own people, but not seriously enough to do something for the millions of Rwandas at risk of violence.

Western nations would go the distance to prevent Western casualties, but were quite happy to step over the African bodies already on the ground and to abandon those still standing. That left me and the skeleton force that remained of UNAMIR, along with a small group of brave NGOs, missionaries and journalists, screaming into the void of international indifference. We were the only outsider eyewitnesses, yet we could not get anyone to believe what we reported.

What mystified me was how the West had failed to learn from the Holocaust. We seemed unable to imagine the ways in which Hutu humiliation under Belgian/Tutsi rule could lead to a similar mass atrocity. Did we think that Africans were somehow more stoic or less sensitive than Europeans? By April 1994, the forces that propelled Hitler to power had been examined and discussed for decades, yet we failed to see the same pattern developing in Rwanda. I believe this complex and sophisticated link between humiliation and resentment never fully dawned on those outside of Sub-Saharan Africa because of an inhuman lack of empathy and reckless disinterest.

Although the African continent had been the object of a colonial-era scramble for control of land and natural resources, as well as the scene of Cold War struggles, by the end of the 1980s, it had been largely abandoned to its post-colonial and post–Cold War fate. Intracontinental massacres were expected (and tolerated), as power vacuums left by the departing colonizers were filled; under the guise of gaining new freedoms, post-colonial countries in Africa were set adrift to deal with the still-raw wounds of colonialism. The breakup of the Soviet Union was creating a multitude of other problems that absorbed bandwidth and resources. And many national armies in the West were already overcommitted to coalition-based operations and UN peacekeeping missions around the globe, as a wave of instability swept over countries that in the Cold War had been stabilized both economically and politically by one or the other major power bloc.

To most outside observers at the time, Africa was a scene of general social and economic collapse, heightened by deadly famines, civil wars and mass atrocities. Western and Northern countries considered Africa a continent to be pitied, not a source of potential; it was certainly not a priority.

In the background of all this was domestic pressure within stable nations to reap a "peace dividend" from the end of the Cold War, meaning a significant reduction of defence spending. In 1991, the first Gulf War demonstrated the capacity of a US-led coalition to confront the national army of a "rogue state." This contributed to a dangerous level of confidence that the military powers of the West could join forces to meet significant threats to the resources that mattered to them—a sign of the "New World Order" US president George H.W. Bush had heralded. (I will go into more detail about this in Part Two under "Status Quo.") But when faced with the reality of what I soon began to call the "New World Disorder" in failing nations such as Somalia, no one knew what to do. American blood spilled in Mogadishu had prompted an entirely new US foreign policy articulated by Bill Clinton in his Presidential Decision Directive 25 of March 1994: the United States would commit troops to an international engagement only if it saw an advantage for American interests.

Another layer to this disinterest was (and very much still is) the West's growing fascination with itself. Even in the era before smartphones and social media, we had already demonstrated an unhealthy fixation on celebrity and a focus on what was happening close to home. My own experience of returning from Rwanda in 1994 to a continent absorbed by the O.J. Simpson trial illustrated just how effectively our media had learned to feed us what they think we want, rather than what we might need to know. I was also hard hit by Amber Alerts marshalling continent-wide efforts to search for a single missing child, when hundreds of thousands of Rwandan children had been slaughtered with barely a blink from the rest of the world. Of course, I don't object to Amber Alerts, but rather to the disconnect. That old saying from the sixties had become reality: "If you don't mind, it don't matter."

Genocide should matter. We should mind.

Further evidence of infernal disinterest from the West was the lack of adequate resources provided to my mission, and the unreasonably short deadlines imposed on it to secure the delicate passage to a broad-based transitional government in Rwanda.

The timetable for implementation says a lot. The Arusha Accords were signed on August 4, 1993. The UN peacekeeping mission it called for was supposed to be in place and in country within thirty-seven days. No one with even the briefest experience in the world as it was at the time could have considered meeting this deadline remotely possible. Yet a failure to deploy on time with a credible capacity would undermine confidence in the peace agreement the negotiators had just reached. Delay would also permit the hardliners who had not signed the accords time to start coalescing plans in secret (which they did).

And even as I tried to meet the deployment deadline, I was actively stalled at every step of the way from within the UN system by staff in DPKO, the Department of Political Affairs and Mission Support Services, all of whom had lots of experience trying to raise missions and knew member nations were unlikely to commit the needed resources and troops at all— let alone under such a time pressure. I was told repeatedly that the peace accords' milestones could never be met, that it commonly took a minimum of six months to raise a UN peacekeeping mission, and much longer to build it to full operational capacity. The logistics side of the UN was run separately from the military operational side, and there was no money or equipment available for new missions. How could it be that no one involved in the diplomatic process that led to the peace agreement was aware of the realities the mission would face? The easy answer seems to be that they didn't want to know—or maybe they genuinely thought that getting signatures on a piece of paper would be enough.

Anyone engaged enough to look at the violent tensions in Rwanda and the steady flow of weapons into the country at the time should have been able to see that the only real hope for peace was to deploy a strong, credible international force empowered with a mandate to prevent violence. Any agreement between two parties separated by so much mistrust needed a competent and capable referee. This was certainly obvious to me and my staff within weeks of arriving in Rwanda, so it should have been obvious to anyone who'd had more time on the ground and better sources of information—namely, France and Belgium and the other foreign embassies involved in the peace process in both Kigali and New York.

The kindest explanation is that these countries wanted a quick solution, but their priority was the conflict in the former Yugoslavia. In effect, hope was all they were willing to commit to the exercise in Rwanda, and to sustain that hope, none of them were encouraged to speak the truth. I was barely able to present an honest estimate of the number of troops I needed—4,500, at a minimum—because I could not gather enough intelligence to make it credible in the eyes of the UN Security Council. Disinterest from troop-contributing nations prevented me from getting even that minimum; I ended up with 2,600, of whom fewer than half had the viable military skills and knowledge to function operationally, even in a Chapter VI mission. They came with next to no equipment; even the wealthy Belgian contingent arrived with broken-down vehicles straight out of their Somalia mission, which needed months of repairs before they could get back on the road.

I have spoken often about the international community's inaction when it came to Rwanda, but it's also enlightening to break that down to the role that individual member states played.

The historical record makes it very clear that for domestic reasons the Americans wanted to be seen to be independent of the UN Security Council. Where once the United States had taken pride in leading the UN, headquartered as it is in New York City, by 1993 the country had turned against the UN, for what they saw as its unwarranted interference with American sovereignty. To demonstrate that he could stand up to the UN, President Clinton withheld funding, particularly from peacekeeping missions. American delegates to the UN actively blocked support for UNAMIR and argued in favour of shutting it down after the genocide began. China was not yet involved in UN peacekeeping, and Russia was busy dealing with its internal turmoil following the collapse of the Soviet Union. The UK played its usual post-empire game of holding its cards close to its chest; with embassies in Nairobi, Kampala, and Dar es Salaam, as well as close ties to the Americans, the British clearly had a great deal of intel in the lead-up to the genocide, yet they shared nothing. (Given the country's egregious history of colonization, this silence seemed particularly appalling.) Belgium was in a complicated position because of its colonial past in Rwanda, and it did not have a seat on the Security Council.

Such interest as there was in intervening to end the genocide by reinforcing the mission came from non-permanent members of the UN Security Council, particularly New Zealand and the Czech Republic, who, after the killing had started, consistently raised questions about the veracity of Rwandan and French government claims. Canada, which had an arm's-length association with Rwanda through church and academic exchanges, as well as large development investments there, had no embassy in Rwanda and no seat on the Security Council. The only non-African nation-state that showed any substantive interest in Rwanda at the time was France, which, as I've already mentioned, was motivated by its desire to maintain its post-colonial grip on the region.

More locally, Burundi was preoccupied with its own factional disputes; Zaire was falling apart under President Mobutu Sese Seko; Tanzania was concerned enough to attempt to resolve frictions in the area but was generally ignored; and Uganda was directly involved in supporting the RPF (if only to send Tutsi refugees back to Rwanda).

There were four impoverished African nations that would send me troops, but no wealthy country was willing to provide them with equipment and weapons, or food, or transport to get them to me. Apparently, there were fears that if they equipped these battalions, the troops would take that equipment back to their own countries, where they would use it to conduct coups. It was appalling, treating these African nations like undisciplined children who couldn't be trusted. Compare that with how the international community is trusting the

Ukrainians to use the tanks, guns, communications systems and bombs we are supplying them with today.

Bureaucracy generates its own cycle of indifference, which had a huge bearing on the capacity of UNAMIR to do what was asked of it. As a career soldier, I thought I knew something about bureaucracy and believed I was ready to figure out and circumvent the UN version of it. I was wrong. The institution that had enacted the Genocide Convention could not rouse the nations that make up its membership to deliver vital supplies, weapons, vehicles and logistics in time to be of use.

The Department of Peacekeeping Operations, Maurice Baril and Kofi Annan especially, did fight to get me resources and troops to stymie the waves of human destruction. But they were constantly blocked by the Americans, and no nation—not even my own country of Canada—would provide us with resources to stop the killing.

Apparently, some humans were simply not worthy of protection under the conventions of human rights that have evolved in the richer nations of the Global North, and which are supposed to be universally applied. Indifference to the urgency and severity of Rwanda's impending fate defeated us before we even started. Disinterest cemented that fate.

SELF-INTEREST

The melancholy souls of those
Who . . . [not] faithful were to God, but were for self.
                              Dante, *Inferno*, Canto III

War—as military theorist Carl von Clausewitz wrote—is the province of danger, and the first quality of a warrior is courage in the face of it. Once it was clear that Rwanda was descending into genocide, courage was in short supply. France, Belgium, Bangladesh and other UN member states evacuated their troops in a startling show of self-interest, self-protection and reluctance to accept military casualties, displaying the opposite of the warrior ethic. They quickly rounded up their national civilian expats and flew them out too, leaving their Rwandan friends and colleagues to the slaughter.

When the head of the United Nations, Boutros Boutros-Ghali, ordered me to abandon our mission, he told me that there no longer *was* a mission because there was no more peace to keep. He said there were reports from Belgium that Hutu extremists were coming to kill us and stressed that "the world cannot accept any more Blue Berets killed." Apparently, the world could easily accept the murder of tens of thousands of Rwandans.

When I refused his order to leave Rwanda, he repeated his command, unused to hearing no. Again, I said, "Absolutely not."

The secretary-general slammed down the phone and it immediately rang again. This time it was his chief of staff on the line, who barked at me, "Do you realize that you just received a legal order from your legal commander? An order to protect your own forces?"

I replied yes, and this time it was me who hung up the phone.

My refusal was an instinctive response bred of my upbringing, my training and the community I came from: my school, my church, my parents, my brothers and sisters in arms. It was clear to me—fundamentally clear—that while this may have been a legal order, it was an immoral one. At that stage of the slaughter, a thousand individuals were being murdered every hour. If we left, the human beings sheltering with us at Kigali's Amahoro stadium and our four other protection sites would die. To ask me to abandon them to save my own skin was profoundly immoral.

So I became a rogue commander. I went to my UNAMIR deputy, Brigadier-General Henry Anyidoho of Ghana, and said, "Here's what it is: I am now here illegally, against orders. Any orders I now give are illegal. It is entirely up to you to stay with me or not."

Without hesitation, Henry agreed, along with 450 troops who also agreed we had an ethical obligation to help where we could and, at the very least, to bear witness. Individual countries may have turned tail and abandoned Rwanda, but we few remaining UN peacekeepers would not. And so, the UN flag continued to fly over my mission headquarters.

However, 2,200 soldiers—the bulk of my force—fled to their respective homes, having been withdrawn by their governments. Thus, UNAMIR lost almost every shred of its meagre credibility and the people of Rwanda were abandoned to their fate by the world community. The fact that we had been deployed and proven useless did *more* to encourage the mobilized Hutu masses than any amount of beer and machetes. Nothing could have been better calculated to demonstrate to Rwandans on both sides of the conflict that, as far as the rest of the world was concerned, they were on their own. The architects of the genocide couldn't have hoped for a better outcome.

Self-interest quickly rears its ugly head when nations are asked to give money or blood to the common good without getting something back. This "what's in it for me" logic undermines the United Nations at its foundation.

Every UN peacekeeping mission depends on voluntary compliance and voluntary contributions from member states. To this day, the DPKO (now called the Department of Peace Operations, or DPO) does not have an annual operating budget for missions, so must raise money from member countries on an as-needed basis. For example, the operating budget for UNAMIR was not approved until January 1994, three months after we had begun to deploy.

While this ad hoc arrangement might prevent the DPO from becoming an instrument of some new form of colonialism, it also makes it highly dependent on the whims of individual nations' interests. If key contributing nations want to avoid commitment, they can—and often do.

During the Cold War, the bulk of peacekeepers had come from wealthy countries—Ireland, the United States, Canada. These stable nations relished engagement in relatively benign Chapter VI peacekeeping missions, where the job was to impose the moral presence of the UN and had nothing to do with the use of force. That backbone dissolved with the end of the Cold War. The messy conflicts of the New World Disorder, which required the use of force, were perceived as too politically risky. Suddenly, responsibility for staffing peacekeeping missions fell to troops from poorer nations (which perhaps had more need of the US$1,000 per month they received for each soldier they sent). Interestingly, Rwanda is now one of the top contributors to UN peacekeeping missions, with a steady stream of six thousand military and police deployed around the globe. As I write, Canada has twenty-seven individuals deployed.

Picking apart France's actions before, during and after the genocide becomes easier when you follow the thread of self-interest. The battalion of French paratroopers who arrived in Kigali within forty-eight hours of the beginning of the genocide may have saved their own people, but they also conveniently cleared the way for the *génocidaires* to operate without the risk that uncontrolled militias might massacre French civilians and shock the French public into paying closer attention to what their government had been doing in their name. It also gave a green light to the plotters who had just conducted this *coup d'état* (though the fact that the new Hutu government was being launched inside the French embassy in Kigali might have done the trick on its own). Given the long history of collaboration with, and support to, the Habyarimana regime, France's actions here looked like an open embrace of the new course the hardliners were embarked upon, particularly since one of the people the battalion evacuated was Madame Habyarimana, the president's wife.

What has become much clearer in the years since the genocide is that France's commitments to Franco-African states had created a kind of neo-colonial headlock that forced the French to continue to support the Habyarimana regime— France's allies in other African states would have been threatened had it stepped away. Given that France had military experts training and working closely with the Hutu RGF and the paramilitary *gendarmerie* in the years leading up to the genocide, it is inconceivable that they did not know about the spate of massacres of Tutsi civilians in northern Rwanda. This suggests France had a strong interest in continuing to support the Habyarimana government—anything less might have threatened the credibility of its African network. Respect for human life took second place to *raison d'état*. Mitterrand wanted France to remain a world power, so it couldn't entirely wash its hands of Rwanda, but it also didn't want to spill

French blood or spend French money on the UN mission there. Even self-interest has limits when it comes to humanitarian involvement.

Self-interest ruled decision-making in 1994—whether it involved abandoning others to horrific atrocities or actively supporting genocide for political gain. This is a shame we all bear. But self-interest is still the leading criterion we use for becoming involved today. Russians were interested in helping the Assad regime in Syria starting in 2015 because it gave them access to a naval base in the Mediterranean. That same year, Saudi Arabia's engagement began in Yemen as part of its securing hegemony in the Middle East. NATO members weren't willing to commit troops to fight in Ukraine in 2022, even to protect a country being invaded by a rogue nation, but because Ukraine borders Europe, they were willing to provide some resources for Ukrainians to fight and die to protect themselves. No one is helping Haiti through their current desperate series of political, economic and environmental disasters. Despite our lofty commitments and proclaimed righteousness, self-interest dominates.

IGNORANCE

O creatures imbecile,
What ignorance is this which doth beset you?

Dante, *Inferno*, Canto VII

The speed of the killing in Rwanda caught the world by surprise, but the world's reaction was also slowed by culpable ignorance. In the beginning, the enormity of what was happening was just too much to comprehend. The pure audacity of the strategy struck some in the West as impossibly ambitious for a "developing" country. How could machetes—so low-tech—possibly kill so many people in such a short time? Rwanda had no trains, no gas chambers, none of the infrastructure needed for industrial killing on the scale of Nazi Germany. The son of France's president, Jean-Christophe Mitterrand, who headed the country's African Cell, was quoted in the *Guardian* as claiming there could not have been a genocide in Rwanda because "Africans are not that organised." Racism and ignorance go hand in hand.

Also, many still associated the word *genocide* with the Holocaust, rendering it unthinkable that it would come to pass anywhere else. If Cambodia comes to mind, remember that its "killing fields" were so named to avoid calling the Khmer Rouge's 1970s slaughter there a genocide.

Similarly, our belief that humans share an innate reluctance to kill prevented us from even considering how effectively authority and coercion can be used to provoke people to murder their neighbours. We knew from the massive graveyards throughout Europe how easily the structures of authority in a nation-state could launch millions of young men over the top of their trenches into suicidal attacks; we remind ourselves of this every November. And still, we failed to recognize (or were kept ignorant of) any warning signs of what was being planned in Rwanda.

When I originally deployed on my reconnaissance mission in 1993, I had only a vague idea of the many actors, both international and domestic, operating behind the scenes. I also had no idea how utterly unprepared both the international diplomatic system and the UN peacekeeping system were to support such a challenging mission, or even to appreciate the gravity of the challenges. Even after my deployment, the parties were still arguing about the content of the Arusha Accords. In hindsight, my lack of knowledge seems to have suited many of those intent on using the UN presence to further their own ends.

In January 1994 I had enough evidence of preparations to wipe out the Tutsi population to send my fax to the UN. But masses of evidence gathered since—by humanitarian organizations, academics and journalists including Rakiya Omaar of African Rights, Alison Des Forges of Human Rights Watch, Howard Adelman, Astri Suhrke, and Linda Melvern, the

International Panel of Eminent Personalities (IPEP), and testimony given at the International Criminal Tribunal for Rwanda, to name but a few—all confirm that those preparations started shortly after the RPF invaded Rwanda in 1990. The option of genocide was conceived *four years* before it was executed.

The information was there in 1993, I'm sure of it, but it was never shared with me. NGOs and UN agencies were supposed to make a synergy, not silos. Or so I thought. But they didn't disseminate the information they had. If only the World Food Programme, UNICEF, the UN Refugee Agency, and the UN Development Programme (to pick random examples) had pooled their information on a potential conflict zone like Rwanda and then shared it, I would have had a substantially clearer picture of the problem. Instead, I felt like I was being led into this potentially explosive scenario blindfolded.

Canada—the peacekeeping darling of the international community at the time—had only one captain assigned to gather intelligence over the entire African continent south of the Sahara. Outside of DPKO staff and desk officers (who were each handling up to three or four missions at a time all over the world), there was no intelligence collation at all. The political staff of the UN provided only superficial material on the complex situation. So I embarked on my mission in near-total ignorance of Rwanda's history and its current political and social structures. This ignorance may be acceptable in a member of the public, but not in representatives of the international community who are supposed to be advancing human peace and security.

And it wasn't just country background that was kept from me. Ignorance was imposed on all UN peacekeeping force commanders during that period. This type of mission was so new, there was no doctrine or training for peacekeepers to draw on. A lack of information of the true state of play on the ground, and its complexity and ambiguity, from politics to security to humanitarian needs, was the norm at the time; no formal intelligence or analysis body existed to create a clear picture. The troops under our command were not those with whom we had trained and fought; we were dependent on the troops that were volunteered from any interested member state, ranging from the lowest-skilled battalions, arriving without a pot to piss in, to NATO-standard equipped and trained former colonialists who behaved like they were still masters of the universe.

Few troops, even among those deployed from other African countries, knew much about Rwanda. We were provided with no interpreters. No intelligence-gathering capabilities. We weren't informed which of the players in the peace process were moderate and which were extremist, who were elite and who were not. We had to pick it all up on the fly.

In 1993, maybe we also assumed we didn't need to know. The West was still a little drunk off its apparent victory over the Soviet Union. When the Berlin Wall came down in 1989, Americans, Europeans, and their allies thought they had proven the supremacy of democracy, respect for human rights, and free market economics. They were blithely ignorant of the quiet ambitions of emerging powers like China, the growing animosity of the Muslim world, and the fragile and fractured complexities of so many newly independent African nations now at risk of massive abuses of human rights. And the US had hidden ambitions of its own.

We in Western democracies thought our values were self-evident and true in the eyes of the whole world. We watched Nelson Mandela walk out of prison in February 1990 and become president of South Africa four years later, and we thought anything was possible. We believed that human rights and liberal democratic theory formed a universally accepted framework for thinking about politics and governance. Though I could not see it at the time, the pressure negotiators applied in Arusha to establish a Western-style multi-party system to share power in Rwanda was absurdly ill conceived as a way forward in a country with zero experience with a democratic system. Far more appropriate, in my opinion, was the system ultimately implemented by Paul Kagame: a slow process of reconciliation and transition, under the firm hand of a benevolent and steadfast leader, that allows the country stability as it navigates toward democracy. If there is no local experience with democracy, multi-party elections immediately after conflict become a source of division and turmoil; they split communities and split power when rapprochement is required. What is essential, at least in the short term, is the familiar.

But in the 1990s, few non-Africans understood the unique cultural nuances throughout sub-Saharan Africa. Embarrassingly, Western education and media were still shilling the "mystery" of the "Dark Continent," an image that left most of us intellectually in the dark. The Africa "experts" of the day (many of whom did not speak the languages or know much about the various histories and cultures) were making long lists of corrective actions that might be implemented to "develop" so-called backward African states. In fact, both Kigali, the capital of Rwanda, and Kampala, the capital of Uganda, were run by well-educated, thoughtful, shrewd leaders.

So, on landing in Rwanda, we were unprepared to grasp the enormous difference between what was visible driving through the countryside (tiny farmsteads without plumbing or electricity scattered on picturesque hilltops) and what should have been obvious from even a cursory look around the wealthy suburbs of Kigali (a sophisticated elite with huge power over the rest of the population). Heinously, we viewed the population as simple people with little economic or political clout, without understanding the enormous source of power they represented—once mobilized—to the economic and political elite living in relative luxury in Kigali. This was not a unique situation; it is a dynamic that reaches as far back as the seignorial period in the Middle Ages, or even farther, when a few people controlled the land, the people, the production, the wealth, everything. How could we be so familiar with this model, and still so unable to recognize it?

As an example, we were not provided with information to glean the enormous impacts of Belgian colonial masters assigning identity cards, imposing an ethnicity on each person, and how this became a tool used to manipulate fear and hatred. As a member of the French-speaking minority in Canada, and someone who lived through the separatist movement that nearly split my own country apart, I was well placed to understand why distinctions between Tutsi and Hutu would have been important to Rwandans. But without a better understanding of the clan system, or of how disciplined Rwandan society was at the time, I could not grasp how easy it was for the country's leaders to create and manipulate factions using distorted narratives originally developed by Europeans erroneously speculating about ethnic origins.

I admit these failings not to excuse them, but to point out again the value there would be in a research body within the UN tasked with studying the world's trouble spots and preparing in-depth briefings and contingency planning for its missions.

I thought I knew why I had been selected to lead UNAMIR. As a Canadian, I was perceived as a neutral party, without the potential bias of an ex-colonial. I spoke French, one of Rwanda's official languages. I had considerable experience in command, as well as leadership experience in preparing troops for classic peacekeeping in Cyprus, Cambodia and Yugoslavia. This all seemed reasonable (and exciting, and flattering) to me at the time.

But I can't help but wonder if I was chosen for more duplicitous reasons as well—first and foremost my lack of experience in Africa. Did that make me the perfect pawn for those who understood Rwanda and how the region worked much better than I did at the time?

Ignorance, in fact, was of great value to the architects of the genocide.

FEAR

For wings could not outstrip the fear

Dante, *Inferno*, Canto XXII

gnorance breeds fear, and fear is a main catalyst to violent
conflict. Fear is also one of the most effective tools in the
arsenal of war. In 1990s Rwanda, the Hutu lived in fear of
being once again subordinated by the Tutsi, the Tutsi feared
persecution and total annihilation, the French were afraid
of American interest in the region, the United Nations was
frightened to act, member states feared taking casualties, local
radio was stoking fears of the "demon" Tutsi, and the Hutu
extremists used fear as a spectacle, a warning, and a weapon.

This cycle of fear and violence began with the ruthless colonization of Africa, and in Rwanda, specifically, with Belgium's
imposition of arbitrary concepts of superiority, inferiority
and difference on the Hutu and Tutsi populations.

Decades of discriminatory favouritism ensued, founded
on European myth-making about the supposed traits of the
Tutsi and the Hutu peoples. Through the first half of the twentieth century, Rwandans themselves grew to believe these
false distinctions. Hutu were deemed too limited to be capable of anything but basic labour or agriculture and, as a result,

were denied access to educational opportunities and locked out of government jobs. This spawned a Hutu inferiority complex, reinforced by the Catholic Church, which also doubled down on Tutsi domination by promoting Tutsis over Hutus within the church hierarchy.

Even as independence movements swept across Africa, the Belgians weren't finished toying with Rwandan identity. By the early 1950s, Belgium had changed. The old idea of "natural order" had lost its credibility, the monarchy had lost its power, and imperialism had lost its appeal. The new crop of Belgian administrators and churchmen began to see the injustice of the system they had created at the same time as the Tutsi elite they had nurtured began to agitate for independence. To buy time, the Belgians found it expedient to undermine this new direction in Rwandan politics by shifting their support to the emerging Hutu parties.

By that point, few Rwandans could escape the roles they had been assigned by their imposed "ethnicity" labels. Ultimately, the propagation of fear and loathing over the seventy-five years from colonization to independence eventually made killing off the Tutsi population seem like the duty of all right-thinking Hutus, just as Hitler had brought his people to believe that the Jewish population was a deadly threat that needed to be eliminated. This thinking also meant that Hutu extremists saw moderate Hutus as traitors—also targets for slaughter.

Identity-based persecution is not a job for a sniper, but for an area weapon. In this case, the weapon was the sense of injustice of the Hutu population en masse. They just had to be brought to the point of believing that they were all victims of Tutsi dominance, and that the Tutsis were all in it together.

Fear can arise from within or be sparked by outside influences, especially trusted authorities. In many rural communities around the world, radio is more than just a medium of mass communication and entertainment, it is almost as authoritative as the word of God. This was certainly so in Rwanda in the 1990s, when the Hutu-backed RTLM began its campaign of hate speech and fear-mongering propaganda. In the thick of the genocide, I saw many people with a machete in one hand and a radio in the other.

RTLM was the most influential station on the air. It played the best music too, which made it extremely popular, especially with youth. Its audience was both well established and devoted when announcers (funded by extremist Hutu businessmen) began their on-air campaign to instill fear of the Tutsi, dehumanizing them and calling for the extermination of the *inyenzi* (cockroaches). RTLM hyped fears of potential food insecurity due to population density (in other words, fewer Tutsi mouths to feed would mean more Hutus could eat) and faithfully reported every friction as the Rwandan Tutsi diaspora in neighbouring Burundi and Uganda began to fight their way home.

Massacres of Hutus along the borders reached a crescendo in 1993, after the first duly elected Hutu president in Burundi was assassinated as part of a Tutsi-led *coup d'état*. The ensuing violence generated a wave of massacres of Hutus and caused hundreds of thousands of refugees to flee the country, many of them to Rwanda. This alarmed the Rwandan Hutu population, and the hate propaganda spewing out over RTLM exacerbated their fear of the Tutsi.

British investigative journalist Linda Melvern, who has reported and published extensively on the genocide, calls RTLM a propaganda weapon unlike any other. "The influence of hate radio," she told me, "must never be underestimated." It was RTLM that stoked fear and hatred. It encouraged the slaughter, broadcast names and locations of Tutsis, and provided advice on the most efficient ways to kill them.

By the time we understood what RTLM was doing, we couldn't intervene in this spewing of falsehoods posing as news, because our mission had no radio capabilities. Nor were we provided with the capacity to jam RTLM's signals, which I requested numerous times, because of UN concerns that to do so would constitute interference in Rwanda's national sovereignty.

On the political side, leaders played on the deep distrust between Hutus and Tutsis to focus public fear for their own benefit. Over decades of conflict, Tutsi attacks were sold as provocations and threats, and Hutus were encouraged to respond by massacring Tutsi civilians, which then led to Tutsi refugees attacking again in hopes that victory would prevent further massacres. If this cycle began as both sides trying to deter each other, it quickly became a suicide pact.

Fear was used by and against the international community too. As mentioned earlier, the Rwandan ambassador to the

UN, a Hutu, had a seat on the UN Security Council, even though he represented the extremist government before and during the genocide. Fear of setting a precedent and of backlash from other countries prevented both permanent and temporary members of the Security Council from taking the courageous (and obvious) decision to expel the Rwandan ambassador from the council.

As I have previously noted, the deliberate targeting and murder of ten Belgian peacekeepers at the outset of the slaughter was calculated to create enough fear in European UN member states to ensure they withdrew both their soldiers and their support. If any other nation had been targeted in such a way, the impact would have been much less powerful (and much less symbolic) than Rwanda's former colonial "master" pulling out.

Let me be clear: those of us who remained were not immune to fear. But bravery is not the absence of fear, it is the ability to feel the fear and act anyway. As a soldier and a commander, I was trained never to allow fear to influence my thinking or actions. If only such training was provided for diplomats and political decision-makers.

While the primary goal of the genocide was to eliminate the Tutsi and their sympathizers, another aim of the genocide's architects was to generate the maximum amount of fear and suffering in the Tutsi population. Once I found someone I could trust to translate the RTLM Kinyarwanda broadcasts (which turned out to be starkly different from the shows they broadcast in my mother tongue of French), we rapidly understood that the *génocidaires* were not teaching bomb making for maximum lethality, for instance. No, they were instructing that Tutsis be destroyed one at a time, largely utilizing a familiar farm tool: the machete. Also, they were encouraging deaths that were slow, painful and degrading, not something swift, such as decapitation.

The killers left the bodies of their victims where they fell to intimidate the citizenry. This tactic was similar to lynching in the US, where white supremacists used public displays of murdered Black bodies to instill fear and assert dominance over the Black population. In both cases, such death dealing served as a form of psychological warfare, creating an atmosphere of terror and submission. It's a technique that has been used for millennia and is still in use today; think of ISIS harnessing the power of social media to disseminate their beheadings of Americans. The goal is always the same: fear.

Introducing fear into settings once familiar and safe—like Rwandan churches, which had offered the promise of sanctuary and were turned into killing grounds—can destroy a community's sense of security, and that fear can last for generations. Similarly, using everyday tools to wreak murder can create a lasting and visceral sense of horror in those who survive. In Rwanda, machetes are as common a sight on the roads of Kigali as taxicabs in New York City. Rwandans are taught to wield the machete at a very young age, to harvest crops and to tame the ever-invasive jungle. So the simple machete became a highly effective weapon of war on the psyche, as well as on the body.

Machetes, used intentionally to maim, served as a tool of

fear. While the sight of a dead body is deeply upsetting, the sight of a still-living person with their brain exposed by a massive slice to their skull instills even greater horror and fear. As does cutting Achilles tendons so victims can't run away. As does the mass rape of women and girls. These methods, far more powerfully than quick assassination, create indescribable and inescapable fear. The ultimate goal was for Tutsis to die, but not before they were put through the most unimaginable horrors, both physical and psychological.

The dehumanizing of the Tutsi was so effective that tormenting them turned into a kind of game for the indoctrinated youth of the Interahamwe who carried out most of the acts. Like cats toying with their prey, they treated watching their victims suffer as part of the exercise. The aim was to frighten and humiliate the enemy, as much as to eliminate them.

OTHERING

The vision of those others evil-born

Dante's *Inferno,* Canto XVIII

n his book *The Other*, Ryszard Kapuściński argues that for the last five centuries anyone who was not the son of a white Christian European was treated as "other." Today, of course, with so many technological advances in travel and communication, we are *all* the "other" to someone.

I am a white male who was born to a Canadian father and a European (Dutch) mother, yet I was consistently othered by the ruling elite in Canada because my family lived in ramshackle wartime housing among the filthy oil refineries of East End Montreal, and we spoke French instead of English. My mother was fluent in German, English, French and Dutch, but my father only spoke French, so that was the language we used at home and at school. To encourage me to learn a second language, my mother sent me to a Cub Scout pack in an English Protestant school. This was in the 1950s, and I was a good French-Canadian boy; as I've often joked, Tuesday nights I went to Cubs and Wednesday mornings I went to confession. Straddling these two cultures—Franco and Anglo—gave me early insights into navigating differences and finding common ground, which I am grateful for. But I also experienced discrimination. The long-standing tensions between French and English that date back to the English defeat of the French on the Plains of Abraham 250 years ago dictated that after I joined the military, the only chance I had to rise in the ranks was by assimilation to the Anglo norm. I did (so fluently that I'm writing this book in English, instead of my native Québécois). Yet I was still commonly called "frog" (a derogatory term apparently referring to the French dish *cuisses de grenouille*, frogs' legs). My tormentors sometimes said it backwards—"gorf"—to try to diminish me even more.

During my nine years of serving in the Senate of Canada, I enjoyed very good relationships with the guards, cleaners, clerical staff and kitchen staff; one day it dawned on me that they were almost all French Canadians, whereas positions higher up in the Parliament Hill pecking order were mostly held by English Canadians.

French and English bilingualism has been a federal law in Canada since 1968, but correspondence and communication from Ottawa is still English text first, with French after. The government requires all federal employees to be bilingual, but proficiency in English remains the unspoken criterion for high-salary, high-responsibility work. It was acceptable for Anglos to acquire the bare minimum of French to meet the legal criterion of bilingualism, but employees who were fluent in French and had only passable English were relegated to low-paying service jobs.

When those who are othered wish to maintain their cultural and linguistic self and not be assimilated, they hope to gain equality through democratic processes, equality laws and human rights. In Canada, the Anglo majority acquiesced to legislation respecting the culture of the minority and the principle of bilingualism. However, the Francos testing that bilingualism in the halls of government had to be fully competent in English, whereas the Anglos needed only rudimentary French. As a native French speaker, I had to write reports and give presentations in English, but my Anglo colleagues could never have done the same in my birth tongue.

Over my thirty years in the Canadian Armed Forces, and even now, all operational orders were required to be made in English. So, as the French-speaking commander of a Quebec artillery regiment made up of French-speaking troops, I was required to provide commands exclusively in English. The reasoning for this practice was that we needed interoperability with allies, particularly the Americans, Brits, and Australians. I could see the point in theory, but in practice it made little sense. Many allied nations were not English-speaking and issued commands in their native language; it would be absurd for them to order direct actions using words the troops couldn't understand. I wanted to know why Franco-Canadian guns had to be fired in English, so I launched a formal inquiry exploring the impact of English as the sole language of command. I was immediately labelled a troublemaker and billed a Quebec separatist rather than a committed member of the artillery corps attempting to make life safer for all troops. Beware: when you try to defend your rights—even in a liberal democracy where those rights are written into law—you can still be ostracized for asking for the laws to be applied.

We are seeing a similar dynamic play out in the United States almost daily, where Black and Hispanic citizens are mocked, subjugated, even murdered in cold blood for demanding their civil and voting rights. For me, as for others, the choice when dealing with this cultural bigotry was to either assimilate as best we could or suffer the consequences of being treated as the "other."

This "otherness" is a source of friction that runs deep in the psyche of those treated as second-class. It is a source of animosity that can lead to extreme violence, and it is always risky to underestimate its animating force. In my youth in Canada, it led to a violent separatist movement that planted over two hundred bombs and resulted in government imposition of the War Measures Act. In Rwanda, it led to genocide.

Othering at its most extreme is so dehumanizing that it makes eradicating the scorned ones seem not only conceivable, but essential. So propaganda to dehumanize the enemy is a favoured tactic of war, ensuring front-line fighters and civilians alike support and sustain the effort. Often, but not always, the propaganda twists some aspect of a true narrative to focus on past injustices, highlighting and distorting atrocities and reinforcing stereotypes. Other times it is just absurd ("So-and-so group eats babies; we must stop them!"). In either case, by making the "other" so unrelatable, so barbaric and such a threat to everything a group holds sacred, any possibility for compromise, even basic empathy, is destroyed.

"It did not at all occur to me that these orders could be unjust," a former German police battalion member who served during the Nazi regime testified at his 1962 war crimes trial over atrocities at the Chelmno extermination camp in Poland. "I know that it is also the duty of the police to protect the innocent, but I was then of the conviction that the Jews were not innocent but guilty. I believed the propaganda that all Jews were criminals and sub-humans and that they were the cause of Germany's decline after the First World War. The thought that one should disobey or evade the order to participate in the extermination of the Jews did not therefore enter my mind at all." This policeman simply could not see the injustice of his acts. Similar thinking justified the trans-Atlantic slave trade and the attempted annihilation of Indigenous populations everywhere from North America to the South Pacific.

In Canada (as in most of the world), the Catholic Church's shameful Doctrine of Discovery was used as moral justification to conduct a genocide against First Nations populations. In the late nineteenth and the twentieth centuries, the Government of Canada snatched children away from their families en masse and placed them in residential schools that functioned more like concentration camps, where these children were subjected to forced assimilation, humiliation and brutal—often lethal—abuse, designed to eliminate or subsume Indigenous cultures and communities. As a Canadian of European descent, I share a burden of guilt for what my ancestors did to the Indigenous inhabitants of the North American continent. We've finally made a start in trying to find a way forward by at least acknowledging that we live on lands that were taken by force, subterfuge and deceit, but I can't imagine how we are to recover from the soul-withering fallout of the hundreds of children's unmarked graves that are now being uncovered on the grounds of those residential schools. Nor can I reconcile myself to the fact that, even today, many Indigenous communities and individuals are trapped in conditions of abject poverty, and we *still* have appalling, discriminatory laws in place (see the Indian Act).

But how easily we become defensive, how quickly we rally around our own national or racial identity, if we feel threatened. How difficult it is to resist the impetus to suspect every member of a group that seems to threaten us. One need only spend a minute on social media to find disturbing and dehumanizing language aimed at political rivals embroiled in even the smallest of fights.

Today in Myanmar, the ethnic identity of the Rohingya has been consistently denied by the state and by government-controlled media; the public have also adopted the official narrative depicting the Rohingya as illegals. The Rohingya have been unfairly labelled as Islamist extremists and are commonly referred to in the media as *kalar* (a racist slur), as well as "pests" and "dogs"—labels that dehumanize them to justify denying them their rights as citizens. The Myanmar military blatantly uses such language to rationalize its murderous campaign against the Rohingya. Even the Nobel laureate Aung San Suu Kyi has refused to acknowledge that the violence against Muslims in Myanmar constitutes ethnic cleansing. These are the deadly consequences of othering.

Long before the nation-state was created, our species moved about in search of better grazing, more water, better fishing and hunting, or to escape plague, famine or conflict. These movements and migrations still go on today, as war, economic collapse, drought, disaster and a simple hope for better lives push people over borders deliberately established as impediments to such movement.

We try to control this ceaseless flow of humanity with citizenship and immigration laws, and with international agreements, all of the regulation resting on the use of categories such as citizen, resident, displaced person and so on. The category of refugee includes people who have fled their home country and are no longer part of a state. Life for a stateless person is deeply insecure because, without documented citizenship, a person has no legitimate home and so may not work legally or move outside of an area designated by a host country.

So when a nation-state questions the legitimacy of the citizenship of some of its people based on speculative narratives about how and when they arrived, it also undermines the certainties contemporary life is founded on: that a person belongs somewhere, has rights and is welcome. When hardline Hutu political leaders began to agitate against the Tutsis, they did not need to look far for historical touchstones they could use to play on the fears of the Hutu majority. Colonial authorities had attributed indigeneity to the Hutu majority (declaring that they were the original inhabitants of Rwanda), while regarding the Tutsi minority as settlers who had come from elsewhere. In the years leading up to independence, Hutu leaders grabbed onto these ideas, both to assume the mantle of victimhood and to arouse deep feelings of injustice over being wronged by "alien" invaders.

By positioning themselves as natives who had been doubly colonized, first by Tutsi and then by European settlers, the Hutu majority could justify violence as a strategy to resist being subjugated once more by the invader Tutsi.

It's clear to me that the "developed" world doesn't make distinctions between African nations, whose borders were artificially imposed, let alone between the legitimately distinct sub-regions of the continent. All they see is a huge group of people living in what they perceive as messed-up systems that just don't work; hence, Europeans and North Americans often refer to Africa in the singular. This kind of sloppy, dismissive thinking embarrasses and appalls me.

I testified in the International Criminal Court's trial to bring the perpetrators of the genocide to justice. The tribunal was held in Arusha, Tanzania—the same place where the peace accords were negotiated. In that courthouse, electricity was occasional and the toilets didn't work. The war crimes tribunal for the former Yugoslavia was held in a fancy court in the Netherlands. I repeatedly questioned authorities in Arusha and in the UN's Office of Legal Affairs about this, and I was told that the conditions in Arusha were the "norm" in Africa. Accordingly, they treated "Africans" as people not desirous of air conditioning, functional indoor plumbing or working courtroom lights. The same kind of othering was also used to excuse not intervening in the genocide in the first place.

Europeans viewed, and often still view, Africans as less "civilized" and use this as the justification for dismissing their concerns and conflicts as "tribal." This revolting attitude disregards the fact that the colonial powers were the authors of most discrepancies between groups, building their local control by always favouring one over others. As much as the international community wanted nothing to do with any fallout in Rwanda, the genocide emerged against a backdrop of international pressure on the Habyarimana government to democratize itself—pushing people who were victims of colonization to let themselves be recolonized by this foreign concept.

I recall a conversation I had with a hardline Rwandan minister who had spent five years in Quebec during the FLQ crisis of the late 1960s and early '70s. He'd witnessed the bombings and the anti-francophone crackdown by the Canadian government. He was experienced and clever, and swore better in French than I did, which meant he had some insight into Quebec culture, yet he asked me how it was possible that a member of the Francophonie (Jean Chrétien) had been able to beat a member of the linguistic elite (Brian Mulroney) to become prime minister in the 1993 election. Having been educated by Catholic nuns and priests who made even children's classrooms places of division and unequal opportunity, he simply couldn't fathom the nature of democracy.

How is it possible, he wondered, that a majority of Canadians had voted for the "other"? Because his country was so far from a democracy, the idea was beyond this educated, sophisticated man's comprehension.

HATE

Accents of anger, words of agony

Dante, *Inferno*, Canto III

Hate is our most dangerous emotional by-product. Fuelled by anger, fear and humiliation, it gnaws away at our insides, growing with every perceived slight until it either is washed away by forgiveness or boils over in an attack. If hate is allowed to grow unchecked, even fostered, there is no limit to the depravity that can result. I've seen this with my own eyes. When a person is deliberately humiliated by someone too strong to be attacked directly, it is common for the humiliated party to lash out at whoever is in reach.

Rwanda under Belgian rule was a perfect environment for hate to build and feed on itself. But the degree of hatred in Rwanda was invisible to most foreign observers until after the killing had started. The speed with which that hate was unleashed was incredible, but the campaign to foster it to that intensity had been slow and steady. It started in veiled speech calling for *uburetwa* to eliminate the *inyenzi* (loosely translated as "community work to kill the cockroaches"), hidden in historical references to perceived past injustices, and shaped carefully by hate-mongering demagogues to focus on an "alien race" who needed to be punished mercilessly. Historians believe that such loaded language was circulating months and even years before the genocide.

Tragically and unforgivably, the international community wasn't interested in listening to these hate-filled conversations and broadcasts, and my mission had no resources to hear them either. No one among my small UNAMIR force understood Kinyarwanda, and as I've mentioned, my request to hire translators was refused. I knew my HQ civilian staff was riddled with infiltrators from the Habyarimana government, so I was unable to trust what they reported.

The international community believed the parties' differences could be patched over with peace accords that required both sides to set aside fear and hatred and to trust each other enough to live and work together. A vain hope.

Just as love thrives on understanding, hate feeds on suspicion.

Though the key figures behind the Hutu hate campaign against the Tutsis escaped the carnage they unleashed, most of them have since been rounded up, tried and convicted for their roles in the genocide. Their trials are a matter of public record, and they revealed a lot about the methods and the thinking behind the messaging. Ultimately, these architects of the genocide deliberately cultivated the worst elements of human behaviour and then harnessed them to murder their own Rwandan brothers and sisters. They succeeded in unleashing homicidal tendencies in core elements of Hutu society, abetted by authority figures who actively encouraged the killing. They did not wish to keep control of it once it began, because the chaos and confusion helped disguise the underlying impetus and responsibility. All they needed to do was stoke the fires with radio messages, free beer and the example of authority figures.

By the beginning of 1994, those of us on the ground in Rwanda could discern the Hutus' profound hatred of the Tutsis and their desire to come to a final solution. I sent daily reports to UN headquarters, but my chain of command remained unmoved, mainly due to the fact that moderate Hutus who held key positions in the foreign ministry were keeping hope of a peace agreement alive at the United Nations. But also, I learned later, the mission's special representative to the secretary-general, Jacques-Roger Booh-Booh, actively undermined my reports by downplaying the information I was providing him. Because he was African, and knew Boutros-Ghali personally, his assessments were considered more credible than mine.

The term *genocide* is defined as mass killing with the intent to eliminate a group of people. In Rwanda in 1994, elimination was absolutely the goal, but hate was the means. A large part of the *génocidaires'* strategy was to instill hatred in young people, whose minds are still developing and whose emotions are volatile and difficult to constrain. The youth militia who carried out most of the slaughter were fed hate by adults. Hatred was the fuel that sustained the slaughter.

Hatred of the Tutsis was so great that not only human beings were destroyed, but also artistic or architectural symbols reflective of Tutsi culture. There could be no solace for extremist Hutus if they could not rid themselves of these hated people, also erasing all evidence of their existence.

This was not a campaign meant to slowly wear down a population, as is happening to the Baha'is in Iran today. Nor was it conducted with the Nazis' clinical efficiency. This was a bloodthirsty expression of hate that generated such a level of violence so quickly that it destroyed almost a million people over only one hundred days.

The hate grew with each act of violence, and it spread to infect others. Hate is a force that, once unleashed, multiplies rapidly and is very difficult to stop, until all of what is hated is destroyed. The international community thought the genocide was a campaign of tribal retribution, but it was in fact a scorched-earth eradication fed by hate.

Today, racist, misogynist and extremist hate speech is alive and well on social media and in online forums, because it is so easily propagated by those loud and noxious few who peddle hate in pithy sound bites. Before the internet, if you wanted to debate a topic, you might go to a university or a coffee shop, attend a public lecture or write a letter to the editor. You would probably not have set off to take on all comers everywhere.

Online, the extremists and trolls feel infinite in number, and their voices are amplified to reach a multitude. Three billion posts are shared daily on Instagram alone. Such a volume is impossible to adequately moderate for hateful, dehumanizing or violent content. But an even more critical challenge is the algorithmic bias that actively promotes polarizing and hateful speech. Add to this armies of bots that spread hateful and discriminatory messages at alarming rates, plus the anonymity that emboldens internet users to say things online they would not feel comfortable saying to someone's face. The trouble, as we've learned, is that online hate doesn't stay online. It often leads to severe real-world harm.

Hate is an aggressive virus. Once you're infected, it doesn't seem to matter how much you spew out; you not only stay infected, but you also become a carrier. We need to remain vigilant to prevent the conditions that allow hate to spread.

REVENGE

And there are those whom injury seems to chafe,
So that it makes them greedy for revenge,
And such must needs shape out another's harm.

Dante, *Purgatorio*, Canto XVII

The desire for revenge keeps wounds raw, worsening them through self-inflicted aggravation. Revenge unleashed also creates cycles of violence that can go on for generations. As Gandhi famously said, "An eye for an eye makes the whole world blind."

The Hutu extremists in Rwanda had been grooming and conditioning the civilian population to seek revenge against the Tutsi for years, just as the Nazis stoked the desire for revenge among the German people in the lead-up to the Second World War so successfully that the genocide of the Jewish community throughout Europe seemed nothing more than duly conducted administration.

Such cold and calculated killing, such moral blindness, seems so inconceivable that many theorists tried to attribute the Holocaust to some sort of collective insanity. The Genocide Convention arose out of shared horror at the enormity of what the Nazis had done. The mantra "never again" signified the world's determination to prevent it happening again. We have failed. Cambodia, Burundi, Yugoslavia, Ethiopia, China and of course Rwanda drive that failure home.

These are not the consequences of mere bouts of inexplicable insanity, but of an almost mathematical pattern of failures that lead predictably to mass atrocity—conducted not only by the state against its own citizens, but also by civilians against each other. If this is so clear to me, with my limited experience, why did the United Nations, whose foundational goal was to prevent another Holocaust, not recognize the combination of fear, othering, hate and revenge-seeking that led to yet another genocide? Was it because of the deceit, disinterest, self-interest and ignorance in which the international community continues to wallow?

The massive number of killings is what stands out most when we think of genocide—millions upon millions of Jewish Europeans, Cambodians, Armenians and so many others. But death count alone does not satisfy the desire for revenge. Revenge demands suffering.

In Rwanda, revenge entailed not just killing but also mutilating, torturing and humiliating victims. I do not pretend to understand the psychology behind this, but I witnessed it thousands of times over. Chopping off the breasts of women and the penises of men and leaving them to slowly bleed to death. Slicing unborn babies out of mothers' wombs in front of their families. Forcing children into such unthinkable acts—incestual rape, fratricide—that a parent would beg for the mercy of death, for them and their children. If the *génocidaires* had lined up all the Tutsi and shot them, the goal of elimination would have been achieved. But the thirst for revenge was slaked only by visible suffering and humiliation.

The Hutu felt such horrors were justified because they were redressing decades of oppression. For thirty years after independence in Rwanda, cycles of revenge played out with regularity. While I strongly doubt that anyone—other than the architects of the genocide—anticipated the enormity of the horror that ensued, both sides certainly expected continued retaliations.

The desire for revenge is a response to a perception of having been wronged or harmed. Treating others arrogantly (as Hutu fundamentalists accused Tutsis of having done) or humiliating them (as the Nazis accused the French, English and Americans of continuing to do after the First World War) leads to a desire for revenge. In Rwanda, revenge-driven reprisals against Tutsi civilians in the years between independence and the genocide created such a powerful fear of an eventual vengeful counterattack that the Hutus were caught in a trap of their own making. Fear of suffering the consequences of their own behaviour drove them to project a desire for revenge onto their victims and made the Hutu prisoners of their own fear.

When you feel you must attack before being attacked, you're stuck in what is called a "security dilemma." One actor's efforts to increase their security and protect themselves from potential threats are interpreted by other actors as threats, prompting them to increase their own security measures—a vicious cycle in which each actor becomes increasingly distrustful and defensive, leading to further escalation and, eventually, conflict.

International relations are prone to such security dilemmas, where countries seek to arm themselves or build up their military presence to deter potential aggressors. However, their neighbours may view such actions as threatening and take similar defensive measures in response. Over time, this can lead to such a buildup of military power and tension that it sparks into conflict.

A similar security dilemma can also develop within a country, particularly in situations where there are deep divisions between different ethnic or political groups. Each group's move to defend itself increases the other group's insecurity, inspiring a counteracting move, up to a point where conflict and violence are unavoidable.

The wars in the Balkans in the 1990s are a classic example of the security dilemma. The breakup of Yugoslavia created deep divisions between different ethnic and religious groups, and each group viewed the other as a potential threat. This led to the formation of paramilitary groups on all sides, which engaged in acts of violence and terror against the other communities. The result was a series of wars that ended only with the intervention of the international community.

Somewhat similarly, after the Cold War ended, Western arrogance about their "triumph" generated feelings of humiliation in Russia and stimulated a generation of leaders who seek to restore Russian "honour" mainly through military conquest. The West restrained itself in response to Russian aggression in Chechnya, Georgia and the Crimea but seems to have drawn a line when it came to the invasion of Ukraine.

While NATO didn't put boots on the ground to stop Russia, the West clearly supported Ukraine's defence with both rhetoric and weaponry. It is possible that NATO's expansion eastward fuelled the sense of humiliation and threat that underpins Russia's aggression. If so, a Western-supported victory in Ukraine will almost certainly generate an even stronger desire for revenge in the hearts of at least some Russians. The worst possible course of action by Western leaders would be to act in any way that increases the sense of injustice in Russia; it would be especially provocative if they were to claim credit for a potential Ukrainian victory.

As leader of the RPF, Paul Kagame issued a directive that zero revenge killings would be tolerated during the genocide, a directive he re-emphasised immediately after the genocide ended, decreeing that the colonialist-imposed divisions between Hutu and Tutsi were over. His message was clear: we are all *Rwandans*, full stop. He understood that the overwhelming generational trauma had to end sometime, and so he drew the line in the sand. It was a tough stance, even sometimes problematic, but Kagame understood the tinderbox of emotions and how dangerous it was, and he managed to tamp all that fear and anger down enough to get past it. Thirty years on, Rwandans no longer self-separate as "Tutsi" and "Hutu," and the country is thriving economically and socially, despite the ever-present threat from tensions outside the country that may regenerate the frictions. Survivors still bear the physical and emotional scars; no one who was alive at the time of the genocide was untouched by the horror. But they have been given secure space and time to let go of the venomous drive for revenge that controlled them, and to process their pain so that next generations need not carry it on.

However, unity is a fragile thing. The revenge cycle can never be broken if the last impediment to healing and reconciliation—denial—is allowed to fester.

DENIAL

No falsehood may the verity defraud

Dante, *Inferno*, Canto xx

n 1994, Germany made Holocaust denial a crime. To date, over a dozen other countries have followed suit. Fifty years after the war, Germany and other countries were still fighting such a ceaseless battle against revisionism, downplaying and outright denial of the Holocaust, they criminalized such actions. Thirty years on, Holocaust denialism is still a constant thread in the chat rooms of neo-Nazis and white supremacists. So it should not come as a surprise (though it is equally repugnant) that there is debate around the smaller, remote and less familiar Genocide against the Tutsi in Rwanda—who won, who lost, who started it, who suffered the most.

Genocide denial is always badly argued and fails any reasonable test of historical accuracy. The idea of a "double genocide" (placing equal blame for the genocide's planning and execution on the Tutsis), or denials that there was any planning at all, are generally put forward by ex-colonialists and their disciples, most of whom were not there (many who were not even born at the time). Their "proof" is often drawn from anecdotes passed on by revisionists, or extracted from the testimony of people who were defending themselves in a court of law. These are creative arguments as opposed to factual analysis.

I do not want to repeat these claims, even to refute them, because I have dedicated thirty years to ensuring that the memory of the genocide stays alive. However, some aspects do require attention.

First, I respect that in the fog of war it was sometimes challenging to clearly see the truth. Mark Doyle—a Nairobi-based BBC correspondent who was one of the most persistent and effective, as well as bravest, reporters covering the genocide—has written, "I must admit that during the first few days I, like others, got the story terribly wrong." He explains that pressure from editors in London to submit balanced reports reinforced his own initial impression that he was witnessing a civil war in which violent atrocities were being committed on both sides.

He was not alone. Part of the problem was that the Rwandan government had effectively mobilized a structured civil defence in ways that disguised the fact that the wave of killings of civilians by other civilians was not spontaneous. It took time, initially, to notice that the civilians holding the machetes were in fact organized and supported by government security and administrative authorities. It then took time for the news out of Rwanda to be believed, in large part because it had been deliberately designed to look like something else by government propaganda and the disingenuous briefings the Rwandan ambassador delivered to the UN Security Council. It is also important to note that at the end of the genocide, Hutu perpetrators fled the country and almost immediately began plotting to persuade the international community that there had been no genocide, and so there was no one to be held responsible for the 800,000 dead. As journalist Andrew Wallis reports, in 1995 the Hutu extremist leadership "rebranded" itself as the Rally for the Return of Refugees and Democracy to Rwanda (RDR), a "moderate, maligned and misunderstood" group who argued that they "truly represented the Rwandan people, and could again be entrusted with the running of a country that was rightfully theirs."

They pushed the narrative that the events of 1994 had been spontaneous. Killings were on "both sides," RTLM had only promoted free speech, and the Interahamwe were civil defence units. Wallis also explains that the RDR pinned responsibility for the killings on the United States and British governments, whom they allege trained and assisted the Tutsi RPF. And that France—as Wallis notes, "the major backer (military, diplomatic, political, and financial) of the genocidal regime"—was merely providing neutral assistance.

The RDR was made up of well-educated, internationally savvy players with a lot to lose. As such they pushed their denial agenda at international conferences, with UN institutions and with NGOs, first claiming that there was no genocide and eventually that it was all a plan of the Tutsi RPF.

In 1996, when some of the main architects of the genocide were arrested by the International Criminal Tribunal for Rwanda, the defence attorneys (organized by Belgian Luc de Temmerman, who had long represented the Habyarimana family) gathered on the RDR's dime to promote the Hutu agenda. Michael Karnavas, an American lawyer who was part of the defence team, said, "I was instructed that the genocide had not occurred, that it was simply Tutsi propaganda, but that if a genocide had taken place, the Tutsis were responsible for exterminating the Hutus."

Who will remember the truth when those who wish to revise history with lies are given legitimate platforms and are allowed free rein online? Will negative views about the present-day governance of Rwanda eventually conflate with genocide denial? Will the outside world continue, forever, to impose itself and its fickle *causes célèbres* on this tiny nation and its people?

Denial is rooted in deceit. It thrives on, and is sustained by, disinterest, self-interest and ignorance. Denial regenerates fear, othering and hate, and the more it is indulged, the more it calls for revenge. Denial is the most cunning and perverse of all the failures against peace because it feeds the perpetual cycle, pushing survivors and future generations back into hell.

PART TWO

PURGATORY

Thou hast at length arrived at Purgatory

Dante, *Purgatorio*, Canto IX

F or the past eighty years—and especially the thirty since the Genocide in Rwanda—the international community has been developing tools for peace while simultaneously investing in weapons of mutually assured destruction and continually allowing belligerents to gain the initiative. When the hellscape in Rwanda (and the world's horrific non-reaction to it) was still fresh in everyone's memory, countries and institutions came together in a genuine effort to atone for the series of mistakes and missteps that had allowed it to rage unchecked. However, these initiatives to promote peace—even at the UN itself—have proven to be mere stopgap measures that attempt to avoid or resolve conflict rather than predict and prevent it, all of them hindered by the relentless workings of national self-interest.

I hope that by calling out here the insufficiencies and failures of truces and the relentless tendency to default to the status quo, which only exacerbates disorder, dilemmas, inequality and irresponsibility, we can consider instead how to adopt new perspectives that align with our current era of social, technological and environmental revolutions. The goal is to ultimately achieve a Team Earth mentality that will prepare the way toward real and lasting peace.

To achieve the peace humanity desperately needs, we must closely examine our current habits of mind: we confuse peace for absence of war, or at least an absence of war that we ourselves are involved in. This conceptual failure keeps us stuck in the status quo, endlessly wrestling with disorder, moral and ethical dilemmas, inequality and irresponsibility, instead of resolving and moving beyond them.

Our current era vies with Dante's vision of purgatory: a state in which we see some remissions of our errors but remain trapped by our failure to rid ourselves of them completely. Like souls in purgatory, we have become aware of the problems that lead to human suffering without finding the means or the will to solve them.

Where Dante's inferno is a series of concentric circles descending into the Earth's core, his purgatory is a winding ascent up a steep mountain. Its inhabitants are stoic and patient (for the most part), but their way is challenging and they are still afflicted by the seven deadly sins. Allegorically, they have the will to move up the levels that encircle the mountain— believing that their struggle and pain will be worthwhile— but they face the constant risk of sliding back down.

Since the end of the Second World War and the establishment of the United Nations, humanity has taken small steps up the mountain toward peace, but we are still mired in the same vices and using the same tools that drop us into the inferno of wars. Each time we resolve a conflict, or sign a treaty, or at least slow down the killing somewhere, we congratulate ourselves that we have achieved peace. Then war flares up again.

At the end of the Cold War, as I've already mentioned, most of the West assumed that a glorious peace had been achieved. It was a wrong assumption and a false hope. Despite trends toward unity throughout Europe, the United States still believed that the bolstering of power with force was the key to peace and security, and it quietly began increasing its military might. In fact, the hope many nations expressed for a significant peace dividend camouflaged the rearming not only of America, but of Russia and China as well.

Many also believed that US hegemony would encourage world peace, but this was decidedly not the case: from 1990 to 2010, US forces deployed in four interstate wars, beginning with Kuwait and Kosovo in the 1990s. The shock of vulnerability from the 9/11 attacks on American soil in 2001 hit the last remaining superpower hard, and the United States became overtly hostile, invading Afghanistan and then Iraq. In all, the decades following the end of the Cold War have been anything but peaceful.

We keep paying for our failings and hoping to purge them. We remain tangled up in conflicts and are continually caught out by new disasters, attempting to catch our breath in the lulls between them. Most contemporary conflicts are recurrent wars, not new ones; 60 percent of conflicts in the early 2000s reoccurred within five years. This is not peace.

The current number of active conflicts surpasses previous records. At the moment of writing, Ukraine is fighting a Russian invasion, Rwanda stands accused of supporting a proxy force in the Democratic Republic of Congo (DRC), Syria is still torn apart by civil war (the Assad regime supported by Russia), Yemen is the scene of vicious factional fighting, the countries of the Maghreb are fighting a set of entangled insurgencies, Israel and Palestine are locked in another bloody campaign of destruction, Lebanon has all but collapsed, Libya is torn apart by violent factions, armed gangs in Haiti and El Salvador are challenging government control, Egypt is unsettled, and America is increasingly divided. South Sudan has erupted into violence, as has Pakistan; the Central African Republic, the DRC, Burundi, South Sudan and Mozambique are all coping with various stages of civil conflict; Venezuela and Peru are struggling to find equilibrium, while *coups d'état* are erupting in Niger, Cameroon, Burkina Faso, and Togo; the Uyghur people of China, the Darfuri in Sudan, the Rohingya in Myanmar, and the Baha'is in Iran are all experiencing brutal persecution. Indigenous populations worldwide continue to suffer the effects of genocides perpetrated against them by colonizers. And more than ninety million people are currently displaced or made refugees because of violence.

International initiatives such as the Universal Declaration of Human Rights, policies on the protection of civilians and on human security, the International Criminal Court, and the Responsibility to Protect attempt to bring order to a disordered world. Though each initiative is distinct in its origin, intent and content, all of them are attempts to change the status quo arrangements between countries and their citizens in order to put the welfare of people above the sovereignty of the state.

Our current system of statehood was born almost four hundred years ago when the Peace of Westphalia ended the Thirty and Eighty Years' Wars in Europe. Westphalia imposed a global system of non-interference in another country's domestic affairs that I believe we have outgrown. Our slavish devotion to national self-determination, the sovereignty of the state, and the inviolability of the borders that separate us—no matter the denial of human rights and commission of mass atrocities going on behind those national boundaries—is what led to the failure of humanity in Rwanda and so many of the conflicts in the long list I just cited.

While purgatory is an essential stage of learning and growing, we have been living in it for long enough. Yet, as long as we don't appear to be courting a global conflict, many people seem content with remaining in this stagnant state. They seem satisfied with the ideas and doctrines we've developed recently, such as the Responsibility to Protect and the Sustainable Development Goals, even though our political and diplomatic powers are so averse to implementing them.

We have built international and regional bodies to advance the protection of human beings and keep individual leaders in check. For a time, coalitions of like-minded nations—such as the UN, the European Union, the African Union, ASEAN and NATO—seemed to be making good progress, even though they were still not able to resolve the intrastate or interfactional conflicts that are so prevalent today. Then, in 2022, the international community neglected to stop Russia from invading Ukraine, despite at least ten years of signs that it was coming. When President Putin threatened to use a nuclear bomb, we didn't call his bluff by sending NATO troops to Ukraine, and so the world fell back into another kind of cold war, once again focused on Europe, once again deep in the superpower mentality, wrestling with the same old scenarios. Given our continued reliance on old tools and outdated thinking, we can expect no other outcome than what we've seen in the past: aggressive actions, remilitarization, nuclear proliferation, alliance-based decision-making and global non-reaction.

I fear we will remain trapped in this period of purgatorial, small-minded, short-term, nation-state-based thinking until we finally acknowledge our revolutionary potential and embrace our common humanity, our oneness with each other and the planet.

What follows in Part Two is my review of our current failings, pulled together in hopes this will offer some wisdom as to how we can cast them off and leave purgatory once and for all.

TRUCE

Suddenly the cloud asunder bursts.
As soon as hearing had a truce from this,
Behold another, with so great a crash.

Dante, *Purgatorio*, Canto xiv

I was driving through mountainous backroads in Rwanda in 1994, on my way to negotiations with the leader of the RPF, when I got a call on my radio. Two of my guys—André Demers (now a Canadian brigadier-general, then known to us as "The Kid") and Major Don MacNeil ("Mama Papa 1")— had been moving Tutsi civilians from the Mille Collines hotel in Kigali behind Hutu RGF lines to a more secure location when their convoy was attacked. We'd carefully negotiated the timing and locations of a short ceasefire in order to get this done, but the temporary truce had gone sideways. Donny radioed me to say that Hutu militia were pulling Tutsis out of his vehicle and beating them up. While I radioed for backup, he managed to defuse the situation and stop the violence, but the militia wouldn't let them carry on. They had to retreat to the hotel.

I share this story to illustrate how far a truce—whether a short-term ceasefire or a longer armistice—is from any meaningful conception of peace. To me these days it seems that true peace isn't even the objective at the end of most conflicts; we settle for a cessation of hostilities rather than freedom from the ongoing threat of violence and oppression. Is it really enough to stay alive, only to live in constant insecurity? A state of truce is constantly vulnerable to the stress of an unknown or unanticipated catalyst. We become so busy keeping these precarious solutions stable, we have no resources left for moving beyond them to lasting peace.

In 1944 and again in 1994, the international community affirmed its commitment to protect all humanity and proposed multiple multilateral tools to do so. Some were inspired, but then ignored. Others were merely sound and fury, signifying nothing. For the most part, such innovations as the establishment of the United Nations and the fundamental concept of human rights, proposals for a rapid response force and security sector reform, and policies on human security and the Responsibility to Protect have provided merely shortsighted solutions and temporary truces. Well meaning, even profound, but ineffectual.

Trapped in a cycle of reactionary leadership, we do not think boldly enough. Or rather, when we do think boldly, we fail to *act* boldly.

In the wake of two world wars, the creation of the United Nations was meant to signal the dawn of a more peaceful age. And although the UN fared better than its predecessor, the League of Nations, in becoming a viable forum and instrument for peace, it has still fallen far short of its ideals, due primarily to the greed, self-interest and power obsessions of the states that make up its membership. Originally, the plan had included the creation of a permanent UN armed force ready to deploy when necessary, but tensions between the US and the USSR prevented such a force from getting off the ground. Instead, as I've outlined, UN peacekeeping efforts ever since have had to rely on temporary missions made up of troops from nations willing to volunteer them.

Conflicts of all types continue to occur, and the interests of the five permanent members of the UN Security Council—China, France, Russia, the United Kingdom, and the United States—often make the desire for "peace" immaterial. These five nations' dedication to their own interests is high, and so too is their influence on the success or failure of a proposed mission. UN peacekeeping operations are, in general, much less likely to go where these five nations have strong political, economic, colonial or geographic ties. Recent research confirms that when the Permanent Five (P5) disagree about a priority, the mission ends up with a narrower mandate, a shorter timeline and fewer extensions. In the rare instances when the five are aligned, peacekeeping missions are far less likely to be so constrained. In the thirty years since the Genocide in Rwanda glaringly revealed all the deficiencies of UN peacekeeping (that is, the dependency on the self-interest of the nation-states that make up the UN's membership and fund those missions), too little has improved.

Since its inception in the 1940s, the UN has managed to provide significant assistance in many conflict zones only after the conflict has eased—even though the secretariat does acknowledge that the preferred approach to lessening human suffering would be to pre-empt potential conflicts. The UN does try, using special envoys and political missions to attempt to defuse tensions. But because of the political dynamic among the member states of the Security Council, the UN tends to intervene in only the toughest cases, sending peacekeepers to countries with the deadliest violence when it is already too late to circumvent it. The UN is about twenty-five times more likely to intervene in a war that has already lasted ten years than in one that is only a year old. Surely, we can agree that this is simply not an acceptable system.

Because we have been satisfied with truce, rather than demanding peace, it is not surprising that the UN has such a limited capability as a peacemaker. The nation-states of this world, particularly the most powerful, seem to have a limitless capacity to find ways around the noble commitments they've made to the UN. Even Western democracies, the presumptive exemplars of respect for human rights, find ways to set aside the spirit of the UN Charter whenever it suits them.

While the UN has been instrumental in providing a context for diplomacy aimed at preventing international conflicts, as an institution it has little real authority other than that loaned to it by individual countries for particular and limited purposes.

It's a shame, really. Effective, well-funded and well-equipped peacekeeping is a very inexpensive way to stop people from killing each other, at least in the short term. This year, the world will spend $2 trillion on weapons and only about $3 billion on peacekeeping. I see this as clear confirmation that nations are not actually committed to peace.

Still, the UN was an excellent first step. I just wish its member states had allowed it to go farther, be bolder, evolve quicker, aspire to be greater. But the UN stands as our only constant global institution dedicated to humanitarian objectives. Reinforced by engagements with international NGOs and other groups working toward peace, the UN has struggled to hold the line of relative security and truce.

But truce is nothing like peace. It's a state of flux, not stability. Though it can provide some security for civilians caught in various crossfires, it is far more often pursued to protect the interests of economic and political leaders. Truce can be nothing but superficial, since it fails to address the always-complex roots of frictions.

The mere fact that nuclear weapons still exist keeps humanity in a state of existential fear, always waiting for an attack; these weapons are an insult to the very concept of human security, of life itself. At present, the world is supposedly in a state of nuclear détente, but that could quickly change. Settling for truce leaves us at the bottom of the purgatorial mountain, where our problems only grow.

STATUS QUO

Ah, why dost thou go on? Ah, why not stay?

Dante, *Purgatorio*, Canto v

A
fter the chaos of two world wars, most of the globe found itself in a period of bipolar stalemate, with the possibility of nuclear annihilation maintaining the balance of power between West (that is, the United States of America and Western Europe) and East (the Union of Soviet Socialist Republics). Throughout the Cold War, the US and the USSR fought minor proxy wars, but successfully contained conflict to these few contested regions.

As the world slowly adapted to a new period of stability, the militaries of the major powers continued to do one thing and one thing only: prepare for war. This was how they had been used to maintaining international order ever since secular nations replaced religious and colonial empires. This was war as defined by nationalism, mass armies, technology and clear doctrine: defence of country, defence of borders.

So the Cold War was "fought" by conducting exercises and drills, and maximizing elaborate intelligence, communications and weapons systems; this is the environment I was trained in. As an artillery officer in the 1970s, deployed in Germany under NATO command, I knew exactly where my gun positions were, I knew where to get ammunition, and I knew where the nuclear warheads were.

While we were aware of some internal conflicts that didn't seem to meet this classic formula, events outside of the European sphere—even the twenty years of the Vietnam War, from the mid-1950s to the mid-1970s—were not seen as serious threats to our own security. Maybe the UN could find some kind of negotiated settlement, or heavy-handed governments could be encouraged to suppress frictions. We in the military kept our focus on a potential threat from Moscow.

Then the Berlin Wall came down, along with the Iron Curtain, and with them fell communism. We felt we had won a war without a shot being fired.

Few had pictured what to do about post–Cold War conflict—if there was to be any conflict at all. It quickly became obvious that we in the military had next to no capacity to adapt to this new scenario. Multilateral bodies like NATO, the European Union, the Organization of African States and the UN found themselves in a new era that they had hoped would come but had never really prepared for. The doves were delighted, but the hawks began to worry that they might be out of a job.

One of the first things I had to do on my return from Rwanda was to appear as a witness in front of Canada's Somalia Commission of Inquiry into what had led two Canadian peacekeepers to beat a Somalian teenager to death. Before I'd deployed to Rwanda in 1993, I'd been in command of an operational combat brigade group; my mission was to ensure that troops sent into the field had what they needed to meet the demands being placed upon them. The inquiry asked me to explain how leadership was taught and developed in the Canadian Armed Forces. The question behind the question was, How could such an unbelievably catastrophic failure of leadership have happened?

Fresh from the new kind of horrific conflict humanity was facing, I was confronted in that moment with the incredible vacuum in our training. We were still following the rules of engagement, doctrine and ethos of a bygone era in which uniformed militaries faced off on clearly defined battlefields to gain advantage and defeat a clearly defined enemy.

General Maurice Baril, who had served as military adviser to the secretary-general and as the military head of the UN's peacekeeping operations in every global hot spot during this time of transformation in the early 1990s, put it this way: the military had stumbled into a whole new era of conflict, but had inherited no tools with which to deal with it.

He was right. Nothing in our educational arsenal taught us how to cope with humanitarian missions where civilians were the main targets.

I became obsessed with the need for a new style of "warrior" who'd been educated way beyond the usual training in the use of force—and who would be better equipped to handle the complex issues of these new conflicts. The officer educational institutions, from the Military College right through to the War College, needed a brand-new, intellectually rigorous curriculum imbued with cultural and even spiritual education that addressed the actual needs of soldiers in the field.

The Canadian Defence Policy *was* updated in 1994, but only in ways to better meet the needs of classic warfare, completely ignoring the unprecedented missions we were deploying in Somalia, Rwanda, Yugoslavia, Cambodia, the Middle East and elsewhere. To Canadian Forces higher-ups, peacekeeping was still just a sideshow; they wouldn't be distracted from their time-honoured preoccupation with preventing enemy invasion. They were victims of status quo thinking, and it was dangerous.

Over the years that followed, I was given a formal mandate to reform the officer corps to meet the challenges of the coming twenty years. I developed a plan to put the protection of civilians—and maybe even one day the *prevention* of conflict—at the centre of our officer training, which would also include a broadly expanded educational curriculum. But my bosses and colleagues were resolutely opposed to such a shift of emphasis, worried that expanding the breadth of knowledge among military commanders would undermine their warrior ethic. They truly believed that requiring officers to learn anthropology, philosophy and sociology would weaken their will to engage in combat when required. They also felt that such "extracurricular" pursuits would reduce the time soldiers had to spend on learning new weapons technology and otherwise practising the arts of war. They remained convinced that the experiential development of the officer corps was the most effective means of mission prep, but the experience they emphasized was all based on classic warfare.*

I remember a three-day-long combat development committee meeting in the late 1980s, an annual event that included all the army generals to brainstorm the future of operational strategy. The generals spent one whole day debating the optimal size of a slit trench. This is how tactical, how insignificant the conversation was; they weren't even considering better tools for digging them. My role on the committee was "head of army equipment acquisition and future research trends to meet the challenges of the revolution of military affairs." The generals allocated me one hour of their time.

This status quo scenario was not unique to Canada. In 1991, at the height of the Gulf War, I attended the British Higher Command and Staff College's operational level of war command course, which teaches senior officers to master a theatre of operations. (I was the first Canadian on the course, and my research assignment was to identify and solve the absence of such a capability in the Canadian Officer Corps.) The college was and remains the leading educational body for senior officers in the Western world, but its teachers were nearly oblivious to new thinking when it came to peace and security. While they were at least starting to perceive the need

---

* I'm happy to point out here that every officer in the Canadian Armed Forces must now earn a bachelor's degree, an initiative that was inspired by my reform work of so long ago, according to General Fred Sutherland, my fellow co-founder of the National Security Programme at the Canadian Forces College.

for special ops forces, they continued to instruct students in classic warfighting, even though we rarely faced classic threats.

Like many other militaries after the Cold War (and, in our case, hastened by the Somalia inquiry), the Canadian Armed Forces was also implementing massive budget reductions, which meant there was no money for the innovation and development of new strategies for these conflicts. That didn't seem like such a dire state of affairs to the mainstream military; they remained devoted to the idea that peace and security, going forward, was best guaranteed by classic tools used in a classic way. They regarded any conflict that didn't fit this mould as an aberration, not a sign of a new era. To the military establishment, foreign civil conflicts were small-scale affairs they needn't trouble themselves with, and terrorism was limited to localized groups such as the Red Brigades and the Irish Republican Army. They did not see the fallout from the destabilization and dissatisfactions of imploding nations as the future norm, nor anticipate the scale of the brutality to come.

And why should they, really, when we'd entered the 1990s taking part in a limited conflict that served to reassure military leaders in the West that classic war was still with us. The Gulf War was a Cold War general's dream: a small map with big arrows and a simple battle plan to execute. Half a million folks in combat uniforms took on the other side's near half million, lining up behind barbed wire and minefields, armed with the most advanced weaponry that technology could provide and generations of training and doctrines to back them up. The two sides beat each other up for a while, and the one left standing was the winner. All went according to plan, at least for the US coalition.

After the Gulf War, a false sense of security fell over the military (as well as conservatives in the diplomatic and even humanitarian fields). Going forward, the military expected that the only modifications to the status quo they would need to make would be, at some point, to introduce a robot soldier, which would become the signature lethal instrument for fighting postmodern war.

The military-industrial complex (principally in the US and China) kept increasing its investments in weaponry and research, creating a new generation of precision munitions that were much more effective against the enemy and reduced their own soldier casualties. The push, in the United States especially, was to maintain a technological advantage over any possible enemy they might face, either across a negotiating table or in a theatre of operations.

And so, rather than accepting the new security scenarios and researching new, innovative solutions to face them, militaries continued to move more and more weaponry into their inventory: more stealth capability, more protection of soldiers, more precision munitions, more special forces and, most remarkably, "more effective" nuclear bombs. As an eventual patron of the Pugwash nuclear non-proliferation movement (formally, the Pugwash Conferences on Science and World Affairs, granted the Nobel Peace Prize in 1995), I found it truly ridiculous that at the same time we were reducing the number of nuclear arms in the world's various arsenals, the military-industrial complex was working to increase their lethality and precision, the result being that the world has ended up with *more* nuclear capability than it had during the Cold War.

Even peacekeeping—which had seemed like such a potentially groundbreaking innovation in security—ended up trapped in status quo thinking.

Canada had proudly touted peacekeeping as the country's primary contribution to global affairs. Prime Minister Lester B. Pearson was instrumental in proffering peacekeeping as a solution to stabilizing the Suez Crisis in 1956; in the decades that followed, Canada became a faithful contributor to UN missions. It gained an international reputation as a peace-keeping force, a status that was underlined when Canada pulled all its troops out of Germany in 1993, after more than fifty years of standing guard against a potential Soviet adversary, and elected not to join the US-led coalition in Iraq for what became known as the second Gulf War. These moves signalled Canada's global focus on peacekeeping over war-fighting. Internally, too, peacekeeping became part of our national identity: Canada the Good. In fact, Canadian psychologist Dr. Adam Montgomery recently defined our "peace-keeping myth" as "a belief that peacekeeping involves simply patrolling a well-defined zone of separation between belligerents and handing out candy to local children." My mission in Rwanda was supposed to be a classic peacekeeping mission devoted to patrolling and goodwill.

The hope in the early 1990s was that in the post–Cold War era the "moral presence" of the United Nations' Blue Berets would keep an effective lid on tensions in smaller nations—many of them newly freed from their colonizers and facing the ethnic, religious, economic and power-sharing challenges of nascent democracies. But what if these relatively new nation-states imploded to the extent of conducting mass atrocities—often due to the divisions within their colonially created borders, corrupt leaders and the continued rape of their resources by "developed" nations looking to satisfy their insatiable appetite for oil, diamonds, rubber, uranium, coltan and other natural resources? What then?

Classic peacekeeping wasn't up to that challenge, but would a Chapter VII mission, which opened the door to the use of force, be able to handle it? Or would the international community have to consider *war*?

Those of us who worked in the 3 Ds—defence, diplomacy and development—were dangerously ill-prepared, both philosophically and logistically, for the disasters to come in Somalia, Bosnia and Rwanda throughout the 1990s, never mind the actions of interstate terrorists such as al-Qaida, Boko Haram and ISIS. And so we blundered into peacekeeping debacles, which quickly turned the world of global security on its head. The doves became hawks, pushing for humanitarian interventions. And the hawks sort of turned into doves, because they were unprepared and therefore highly reticent to deploy troops in complex and ambiguous scenarios that did not fit their knowledge base, skills, equipment, tactics or doctrine.

President George H.W. Bush had made that promise: the end of the Cold War would usher in a New World Order. What we stumbled into, instead, was a New World Disorder, wildly exacerbated by our inability to see beyond the status quo.

DISORDER

Confusion and dismay together mingled

Dante, *Purgatorio*, Canto XXXI

The international community, and especially its Western security forces, entered the 1990s filled with a confidence born of thousands of years of military experience, the comfort of almost four-hundred-year-old protocols, fifty years of international agreement, and an expectation of peace. What we encountered, however, was a decade of dirty conflict; neither war as we understood it nor peacekeeping as we expected it.

In early 1993, I had 5,200 Canadian troops under my command, but I wasn't clear who the enemy was. I had a battalion commitment of over 600 troops in a classic peacekeeping mission in Cyprus, but I was preparing over 3,000 troops for missions to Bosnia and Herzegovina, Cambodia, and Haiti. Neither I nor anyone in the military had any idea of what training or guidance to provide the soldiers (or the diplomats and humanitarian aid workers) going into these fluid, dangerous situations. All we had for reference was classic Chapter VI peacekeeping.

In the early 1990s, British academic Mary Kaldor introduced the concept of "old wars" and "new wars" to describe the changing nature of armed conflict in the post–Cold War era. Old wars, she wrote, were fought primarily between states, whereas new wars involve a variety of non-state actors, including warlords, private militias, criminal organizations and military contractors. Old wars were often fought over territorial disputes or ideological differences, whereas new wars are more likely to be fought over control of resources, such as diamonds, oil or drugs. Old wars were characterized by large-scale battles and the use of conventional weapons, whereas new wars often involve guerilla tactics, terrorism and the use of small arms (often in the hands of children). Old wars tended to have a clear distinction between combatants and non-combatants, and most of the casualties were military personnel. In contrast, new wars often have a significant impact on civilian populations, and most of the casualties are non-combatants. These new wars are more complex, fragmented and difficult to resolve than old wars, and they desperately require new approaches and strategies.

The post-1945 world order marked the end of colonialism, but during the Cold War newly independent nations rapidly allied themselves with the US or USSR. They received patronage, which maintained them in relative stability. The end of the Cold War saw immediate instability and even failure of many states; colonial powers had never prepared for the transition to local leadership. As cruelly as they had taken them over, the colonial powers abandoned their former colonies to predictable disorder.

In 1991, Martin Van Creveld, an Israeli military historian, published *The Transformation of War*. He may not have been a prophet, but he came pretty damn close when he wrote:

> Over the last few decades, regular armed forces—including some of the largest and the best—have repeatedly failed in numerous low-intensity conflicts where they seemed to hold all the cards. This should have caused politicians, the military, and their academic advisers to take a profound new look at the nature of war in our time; however . . . time and time again the losers explained away their defeat by citing mitigating factors. Often they invoked an alleged stab in the back, blaming the politicians who refused them a free hand or else the home public which did not give them the support to which they felt entitled. In other cases they thrust their head in the sand and argued that they were defeated in a political war, psychological war, propaganda war, guerrilla war, terrorist war, in short anything but war properly speaking. . . .
>
> Just as no Roman citizen was left unaffected by the barbarian invasions, so in vast parts of the world, no man, woman, and child alive today will be spared the consequences of the newly-emerging forms of war.

What Van Creveld hadn't anticipated was non-state actors bringing the New World Disorder to American soil, on September 11, 2001. They hit not only at the heart of its capitalist system by downing the Twin Towers of the World Trade Center, but also attacked the Pentagon, the foremost symbol and headquarters of the American military. This unprecedented terrorist attack provoked a serious reaction in the UN Security Council, prompting resolutions that condemned it and opening the door to military action. It also prompted the United States government to pass the Patriot Act, which allowed aggressive intrusion into its own citizens' privacy, suspended habeas corpus, breached their civil liberties, and loosened the laws protecting citizens from arbitrary arrest. Canada followed suit to some degree.

The Patriot Act was intended to make it easier for intelligence and law enforcement services to collaborate to protect Americans against terrorist attacks. It also allowed surveillance of private activities without probable cause, which opened the door to abuse. Other changes to government policy—notably the use of torture and a system of international black site prisons—trampled on international humanitarian law in the name of self-defence. Sweeping increases in police powers during that period had bipartisan support, as well as broad popular support. The government of the day had free rein to give police and intelligence services special powers to "fight back" against the potential threat of terrorists. The broad use of the word *terrorist* swept many in the US and worldwide into a wide net. It was a short step to the abuses of Abu Ghraib, Guantanamo Bay, and overflowing prisons.

The chaos and disorder that terror incites is contagious. I found it incredible to witness the speed with which hard-won international agreements and even constitutional guarantees pertaining to the protection of human rights were set aside in the name of collective defence. The 9/11 attacks worked at a symbolic level that was far more significant than the number of people killed (2,996). Ten times more people are killed by gun violence in the United States every year—over 33,636 in 2001, rising to 48,830 in 2021—yet no government body is doggedly pursuing gun reform. Far be it for a federal agency to traduce an American citizen's right to bear arms.

However, the images from 9/11 were so unimaginably startling they created a collective sense of vulnerability. The effect on the American psyche of these attacks on American soil is almost impossible to calculate. Most countries have experienced war, conflict and bombs, but America's geographic (and psychological) isolation had led its citizens to believe they were immune to threats from outside its borders. They were shaken to their bones, as their fundamental belief in themselves as defenders of liberty worldwide was assaulted. And so they overreacted against a collective of perceived enemies, using a catch-all term to describe them: the Axis of Evil. And many other countries bought into this idea and responded in the same way.

No effort was made to open dialogue with al-Qaida; the US just went right off to war. In the words of President George W. Bush, these "Islamic terrorists" were "evil doers . . . who hate our freedoms and our way of life." In the eyes of the US citizens who believed him, the attacks were not motivated by what the terrorists viewed as American arrogance and indifference to their suffering after the Gulf War, or to the values Muslims held sacred, but by pure malevolence.

A terrorist attack like 9/11 can be seen as a sign of rampant disorder or as an attempt to send a message. The message to

Americans? Because of the anger their behaviour had provoked in the Arab world, they were not safe in their own
house. The message to al-Qaida supporters? They were not
powerless. American ears heard the part about not being safe
at home, but not the part about their own behaviour provoking the attack. Instead of seeking to de-escalate through dialogue and an appeal to international law, the US lashed out
with military might, first in Afghanistan and then in Iraq,
labelling both countries as sponsors of terror. What this said
to al-Qaida and its supporters was that their message would
be shouted down, not listened to.

My own country—that bastion of "peace, order and good
government"—had also been quick to suspend civil rights in
response to domestic terror, enacting the War Measures Act
in October 1970 to deal with the escalating actions of the
FLQ. We in the Canadian Armed Forces were soon deployed
throughout Quebec. Major cities, including Montreal and
Quebec City, were under tight police control, and mass arrests
swept up nearly five hundred suspects, most of whom were
subsequently released without charge. The sight of soldiers in
the streets was shocking to Canadians, but it was successful
in deterring future terrorist actions. At the time I was a young
artillery officer commanding deployed troops that had been
sanctioned to use lethal force against my own people, and I
retain vivid memories of the generalized disorder.

In the example of the United States post-9/11, the Americans' extreme reaction to the attacks may have reduced the
number of foreigners flying planes into buildings. But it did

so at the cost of establishing a militarized police state that did little to protect itself and its citizens from domestic terrorism committed by white supremacists, misogynists and every other home-grown hate-filled rogue actor and militia. The long border between old allies and friends, the United States and Canada, became highly restrictive—an interesting juxtaposition to the coming together at the same time of formerly bitter adversaries into the European Union.

Are you, in fact, "winning" a so-called war when you are messing with the fundamental principles you should be upholding? Will we confront belligerents with our rules, rights and laws, or deal with them by bending or even breaking such guardrails? Under the guise of self-protection, the US experimented with severe rule breaking when it came to its enemies, transgressing against the freedoms and civil liberties of its own citizens. Canada, too, faltered when we allowed a fifteen-year-old Canadian boy (born in Toronto but caught up by his father in a battle against American soldiers in Afghanistan) to be detained without trial, tortured and left to rot for years in the seemingly lawless US detainment centre at Guantanamo Bay.

Was it ethically and morally correct to open the door to torture in order to defeat a very complex enemy? When a child is held and tortured as a terrorist, do we allow pulling out fingernails or just toenails? Just exactly how many doors do we allow to swing open, and how do we close them again afterward? When do we return quashed civil liberties to our citizens? Until we do, are we just as bad as the bad guys?

These are just some of the questions of the New World Disorder. When I served as a Canadian senator, from 2005 to 2014, I repeatedly posed them to the country's parliamentary committees, to no avail. They haven't been answered yet.

DILEMMAS

Therefore bequeathed they Ethics to the world
Dante, *Purgatorio*, Canto XVIII

T he New World Disorder brought with it ugly, unfamiliar conflicts and, with them, ugly, unfamiliar weapons. Over the first two decades of the twenty-first century, belligerent terrorist organizations such as al-Qaida, Boko Haram, ISIS, the Interahamwe and the Janjaweed—to name but a few—managed to successfully meet high-tech missiles, lasers and drones with crude and cruel simplicity: Passenger planes flying into skyscrapers. Live beheadings online. Mass kidnappings of schoolgirls. Children with machetes. The terror of unpredictability.

Since the end of the Cold War, there has been an increase in the incidences of ethnic cleansing and genocide, intrastate conflict, forced migration and international terrorism. Laws and conventions that took centuries to build have been thrown by the wayside. Taboos have disappeared, and barbarism and savagery against civilian populations have become common instruments of war.

Specifically targeting civilians in new dirty wars is a technique used to overwhelm and control populations as well as enemy combatants. Not by coincidence, these techniques are reminiscent of those imposed by colonialists on native populations. The targeting of civilians was at the core of the imperialist agenda, turning Indigenous populations into inhuman instruments of labour, using and abusing civilians as leverage to gain power and resources, and inflicting horror as a means to control them.

Once the global balance shifted away from the major powers at the end of the Cold War, smaller nations and groups were at liberty to let loose their imaginations without the burden of conventional oversight. The rules of war and international agreements were worse than irrelevant; they actually defined the limits the belligerents pushed beyond. A UN declaration designed to protect one group showed rebels what would most upset the signatories.

One of the reasons for the success of these shocking techniques—the most heinous of which is the recruitment and use of children in armed conflict—is their effect on the individuals whose job is to confront them. Professional soldiers are taught to follow and to accept the rules of war, training that often leaves them ill-equipped and unprepared to face situations so far outside their moral compass. In the aftermath, soldiers live with the consequences of their actions through the psychological operational stress injuries they incur.

Even today, thirty years after I had the barrel of an AK-47 shoved up my nostril by a drugged-up pubescent child, troops are rarely provided with basic preparation and de-escalation techniques to meet such a threat. After decades of using the NATO lexicon in which I myself was trained and that all professional solders understood ("attack," "defend," "withdraw"), we were tasked with the nebulous goal of "establishing an atmosphere of security." As a force commander, I was left to decipher what this meant. Does "establish" mean your job is to take on and neutralize belligerents? If that's the case, to what extent do you push the rules of engagement? And what exactly is an "atmosphere of security"? Is it a police state where only the police and the army have weapons? No one knew, from strategic commanders down to the tactical level of operations, leaving service members to swim in a sea of uncertainty as they faced situations they'd never imagined.

As peacekeepers encountered new moral, ethical and legal dilemmas in the field, bereft of direction, escalating numbers of them suffered what we now term "moral injuries." In the 1990s, and even to a certain extent to this day, we in the military didn't have the words to name and explain these injuries and knew even less about how to deal with them. Soldiers suffered not only from their injuries but also from the stigma with which the military treated anyone whose wounds were psychological. Governments and militaries were slow to react with programs to rehabilitate these casualties, and the suicide rate among afflicted veterans soared.

In the postmodern New World Disorder, ambiguity and complexity are the norm. Soldiers in the field are forced to try to answer questions on the fly that are best suited to philosophers, anthropologists and ethicists, with no preparation, no training, no lexicon and no doctrine to rely on. Child soldiers. Mass rape. Slaughter of civilians.

The ethical choices facing most of us lucky enough to live in relatively stable societies are usually not dramatic. When we know what is expected of us, we do as the situation requires. Still, even if we do everything expected by our family, church, regiment or country, things can end up going horribly wrong. Think of the sanctimony and violence of white rioters during the 1908 anti-Black Springfield massacre in the United States, or the widespread support for residential schooling of Indigenous children in Canada for most of the twentieth century. Or the many German citizens who informed on Jewish neighbours or helped load them onto trains to extermination camps during the Nazi regime. Or more recently of a Florida governor receiving widespread support, even laughter and applause, for the "joke" of shipping migrants north to the doorsteps of the privileged residents of Martha's Vineyard. To live an ethical life anywhere in our times means navigating between loyalty to the systems that preserve order and loyalty to our own sense of when such a system goes wrong. When called upon, we must be brave enough to stand firm and resist the push of the herd.

To be a soldier is to inhabit a purgatory of choices between equally bad outcomes. Ultimately, soldiers in a combat or peacekeeping environment will find themselves in a position where they must either pull a trigger or not. The complex chain of decisions that brings a soldier to this moment has no bearing in that instant. All they can do is act or not act.

I have struggled for years with the memory of having that child soldier put his loaded gun in my face. Was I supposed to kill that child to save my skin, or accept my own death because the child was too young to be held responsible for his actions? As it turned out, he was easily distracted by the chocolate bar in my pocket; sometimes, sheer luck is as important in guiding ethical action as philosophical theory.

Soldiers frequently find themselves caught between two systems of thought—for example, the warrior ethic and their moral compass—that are each legitimate in different ways. The chance of moral injury is massively increased when they are forced into scenarios they are not prepared for, like facing a child with a weapon.

In Rwanda, I had under my command a young sergeant with a couple of young children of his own at home, who was moving toward a village he had seen people fleeing from. By the time he got there, it appeared that everyone who hadn't managed to escape had been slaughtered. As he was taking stock of the causalities, the doors of the village church opened and about 150 men, women and children came out.

He was shocked: by now, he knew that churches were often used as killing grounds, yet somehow these people had been passed over. My sergeant radioed HQ to request a convoy to transport them to a protected site. As he was making the call, though, about thirty boys appeared at the edge of the village and opened fire on him, his troops and the civilians they were protecting. As he was reeling from that assault, about twenty girls, from nine or so to perhaps sixteen, some of them pregnant, emerged from the bush on the other side of the village and came toward him—they were being used as human shields by another group of armed boys, who also began firing on his position. He was taking casualties fast and had nanoseconds to decide what to do. He understood these were children, ruthlessly recruited into adult conflicts, coerced and violated. Yet his soldiers and the people he was trying to protect were dying.

What *is* the right decision? Regardless of what a soldier in that position does, if he survives, he will spend the rest of his days hearing the bullets flying, feeling his finger on the trigger, seeing the heads of children explode.

The "success" of these weapons of war—child soldiers, mass rape, terrorism, forced displacement—is evident in their visceral effect on the unsuspecting soldiers and civilians who are their victims.

I consider it a profound failing that I made it through three decades of intense military training and experience, only to face so many ethical dilemmas for the first time in the field in Rwanda. Though I had been taught how to cope with displaced persons during NATO exercises in Germany, I had not been prepared for the massive scale of the refugee crisis in Rwanda. Not to mention that unlike in my European drills, there was little to no infrastructure we could utilize in this very real crisis. In Rwanda in 1994 we couldn't raid a supermarket for food. We couldn't open a fire hydrant for water. Out of a total population of 8 million, 2.2 million refugees were forced into neighbouring countries, 1.7 million people were internally displaced, there were 800,000 rotting corpses spreading cholera, and an estimated 30 percent of the population was already infected with HIV.

I would get daily calls from the humanitarian aid warehouses in Geneva and Rome, asking me for updated estimates of the number of displaced people and their locations. (While they kept asking for assessments, they never sent me anything to aid these people.) I responded as best I could, but when I requested photo satellite imaging to pinpoint where groups of over ten thousand were camping each night, I was denied. I was told such an expense "wasn't in my budget." I then requested aerial imaging from countries I knew had satellite capabilities: the Americans, the French, my own Canadian government. They refused, saying these images were classified and sharing them would compromise their operational advantages and interfere with the sovereignty of the Rwandan state. (Was there no extreme of suffering that overrode respect for arbitrary borders on a map?) When I sent out patrols to find out where the internally displaced people were and where they were headed, the patrols were ambushed and I sadly lost good men. How were we to feed these people each day, twice a day, indefinitely? I finally said to just send me enough food and medical supplies for four million people for the next few months. But such support kept being delayed and delayed by a faraway bureaucracy.

As the killing was ramping up, I travelled by UN vehicle to meet with three leaders of the militias at the interim government's headquarters in Kigali. They actually had blood on their hands as I negotiated with them about options for moving civilians between lines. They leaned over the map, saying, "Yeah, we'll stop the killing here for two hours," discussing the slaughter of people as if it were just a simple administrative barrier to navigate. Was I right to sit and negotiate with them? Or should I have grabbed a pistol and shot them? International law certainly didn't permit me to kill them outright, but did that law still apply to an enemy who flouted it so flagrantly?

And what of the people who put us into these situations? Are they faultless? Are they ethical? Certainly, the Security Council of the UN is constantly faced with many difficult ethical choices. The Charter of the United Nations places a heavy burden on its fifteen member states to decide courses of action that will further the cause of peace. To assist in making these difficult decisions, they draw on a huge network of agencies to inform them and on numerous policies, principles and precedents to guide them.

However, their decisions are deeply political and, as I've already pointed out, tied to calculations of self-interest and avoidance of risk of casualties to their own troops. That is just the nature of representing a nation-state at the UN: delegates are not permitted to make detached ethical decisions; they must represent the interests of their member nation within existing political realities informed by domestic politics at home, international alliances and trade arrangements, and their personal status within the chamber.

We have already touched a bit on the troubling privilege of the five permanent members of the Security Council. The P5 have veto powers, so they can block any resolution. Three of the P5 nations are Western democracies with capitalist economies, but China and Russia follow different paths. The other ten members of the council are appointed for two-year terms, and so must guard their reputations carefully, seeking opportunities to further national interests through delicately built alliances. Decisions taken in this context are wide open to influence from vastly different value systems and interests. Few council seats are occupied by philosophers willing to debate principles on their own merits; most are occupied by skilled diplomats seeking ways to preserve or further the aims of their own states, within the broad boundaries set by their commitment to the UN Charter and the Universal Declaration of Human Rights.

In 1998, American president Bill Clinton apologized for his country's lack of intervention in the genocide. Other nations have made similar apologies. And while sound, ethical decision-making at the right moment would have made these meagre apologies unnecessary, the UN Security Council continues to send peacekeeping missions into conflict zones without taking full ethical responsibility for the mission's success. The UN Secretariat continues to deploy teams without providing even the minimum of support, due principally to member states refusing to participate in these most-worthy humanitarian causes. This practice is, itself, unethical. And until these shocking deficiencies are corrected, individuals on the ground will continue to be forced to navigate using their own moral compasses, often with catastrophic results.

The UN isn't the only structure responsible for responding to ethical dilemmas, nor is it only imploding countries that are engaging in ethically questionable activities. Legal but deeply unethical structures, laws and behaviours abound in many communities, nations and international organizations. Immoral systems—whether lawful (apartheid, industrial pollution) or illegal (child labour, political corruption)—are today being questioned and dismantled by highly informed and engaged generations of global citizens. But what will replace those systems? What will guide future ethnical behaviour?

When we send our troops off on peacekeeping or peace-making missions, we expect them to act according to ethical guidelines. We expect our leadership to consider ethics over self-interest in their decision-making. But fundamentally, there is just one question we need to answer as a global community before we touch on any of the others. I repeat: Are all humans human? Or are some humans more human than others?

INEQUALITY

Unequally in anguish round and round
And weary all

Dante, *Purgatorio*, Canto XI

*A*re all humans human, or are some humans more human than others?

This may sound like a shocking, even ridiculous, question to ask. But of all the questions that plagued my mind and my soul after the genocide, this was the most galling, the most appalling, the most horrifically simple. I keep asking it again and again because the world answers it in ways that so often take me by surprise.

We have talked a lot about human rights over the past seventy years, but do we really believe in them? Do we truly believe all humans are human?

This is a story I have told before, but I hope it illustrates the depth of the problem. During the war in Rwanda, extremists used young children to block the roads that humanitarians were using to move water, medical supplies, food and oil. The children did as they were ordered or they were killed. When the aid convoys stopped to avoid harming the children, extremists would ambush them and steal what they needed to sustain the ongoing slaughter.

About the sixth or seventh week of the genocide, as I was driving through no man's land to negotiate the safe transfer of civilians between the lines, I noticed a little boy up ahead, about six years old. Anticipating an ambush, we slowed to a stop. When the child ran off and nothing else happened, I jumped out with a couple of soldiers to make sure he was safe and cared for.

We found him in a nearby hut, sitting among the decomposing bodies of his family. His stomach was bloated and flies buzzed all around him. I picked him up and looked into his eyes—this child of genocide—and I saw the eyes of my own six-year-old son. Here was a boy just like my son but with nothing but horror around him.

What burned me like a torch in that moment was the response I'd received to my requests for help in the early days of the genocide. I've already quoted it, but here it is again: *The only thing here are human beings, and there are too many of them anyway.* And so, the only true criterion for intervention—safeguarding living human beings—had not carried enough weight to win the argument.

No one came to our aid until the genocide was over and almost a million dead bodies lay rotting in fields, in huts like the one where I'd found the boy, in churches, on roadsides, and dumped into latrines, lakes and rivers.

A major reason for this catastrophic abandonment was that the rest of the world saw the people of Africa as somehow less deserving, less sophisticated, just less. This vulgar attitude (whether conscious or unconscious) has led the Western world to become desensitized toward trauma in the Global South. It's a pecking order, as I've said, in which Africa—in particular, sub-Saharan Africa—is at the bottom.

We entered this new millennium with preventive instruments to address complex situations. International covenants and international law articulate and formulate tools we can use to go after the really bad actors, even when their own states choose not to pursue them. And yet, we are not prepared to risk our own troops' lives in countries that do not serve our self-interest. Rwanda had nothing to offer but human lives, and so no one came.

Throughout the 1990s, it became abundantly clear that 20 percent of the world had categorized the other 80 percent as those they will not move to help. We have camouflaged racism with self-interest—subjugating populations so we can grab valuable resources, withholding intervention in humanitarian disasters—exactly like the colonial powers did before us. We say we believe in human rights, but we don't apply them evenly within our own borders, let alone outside them.

We saw it in the response to Rwanda versus the response to the fighting that tore apart the former Yugoslavia, and thirty years later, we are seeing it again. Money poured into Ukraine to help it fight the Russian invasion, but nothing went to the war in Tigray. An emergency visa was created to aid Ukrainians fleeing to safety in Canada, pushing desperate applications from Africa and South Asia to the bottom of the pile. I'm not saying we shouldn't have offered aid to Ukraine, just that our willingness to help in that struggle shines a strong light on our indifference to the plight of others equally at risk.

It is worth considering—at least in hindsight—the forces that have brought us to today's state of deep inequality. The international community sent peacekeepers into the 1990s with the expectation that we would face situations we had encountered before and knew how to handle. What we found instead were pent-up rage, discord and chaos, which have gained momentum every year since.

We found incredible overpopulation. Rwanda, home to 8.3 million, is about twice the size of the province of Prince Edward Island, whose population is 156,000. Can you imagine standing on the Confederation Bridge to PEI as four million people move over it who all need to be able to survive on that small island? Along with overpopulation, we found poverty— unimaginable poverty. Eighty percent of humanity lives in extreme poverty that feeds deep-seated resentment over gross and grotesque inequities, sustains rage, and fuels extremism. To put this in context, just think of how Europe and North America panicked when they fell victim to extremist terrorism, sacrificing civil liberties, human rights and international conventions to try to counter the external threat. (The knock-on effect of all these moves was to embolden internal extremism, especially among those who had once subjugated others and now longed to be "Great Again.")

With communication technologies now so easy, cheap and ubiquitous, even the most isolated places in the world are exposed to global inequalities. Such awareness hasn't lessened those inequalities but has amplified them. The disadvantaged worldwide—Indigenous populations in the Americas, women in the Middle East, youth throughout sub-Saharan Africa— are more and more aware of how they have been abused, of how poorly they have been and still are being treated. While these technologies are allowing us all to see disparity, our awareness is more focused on being enraged by it, rather than fixing it.

Inequality appears to be the fundamental condition of our era; flagrant greed is on the upswing. The wealth of bil- lionaires surged during the COVID-19 pandemic, as energy and food prices skyrocketed, stressing the poor even further. According to Oxfam, one of the world's richest people paid about 3 percent personal income tax in the same year as a flour vendor in Uganda paid 40 percent. Economic globalism has shifted more people to the extreme ends of the wealth and poverty scale, and the distance is growing. Youth are defeated—despairing to the point of suicide—because of the insurmountable inequities they see daily on social media.

More than 50 percent of the world's population is female. Yet this half of humanity (never mind being the source of our very existence) has never been considered as equal by men. Despite some strides, men still dominate in politics, business, academia, the arts and the sciences, binding us within the limitations of male ego, male analysis, male privilege, male- centred knowledge and outright misogyny.

You see so much hatred of women unleashed online, but this is an age, too, of growing female fearlessness. I have to believe that women will soon succeed in loosening the hold men have had over humanity, that iron grip nurtured by religious, social and economic structures designed and built by men.

For many men, this is a terrifying prospect; by "allowing" women to gain authority, they lose their positions of privilege. So they will fight like hell to foster inequality. Backlash in many Western countries is rampant. Therefore, women must not wait to be "allowed" authority and equality; they must take it. I am gladdened to see in my own country, and many others, young women refusing the status quo, and young men, too, acknowledging that the way old-fashioned thinking, traditions and structures have been allowed to dominate is not acceptable. It's worse than unacceptable: it's holding us back.

Gross inequality traps us in ceaseless purgatory. It is harmful, it is disadvantageous, and we all—as individuals, as societies, as humanity—have a responsibility to correct it.

IRRESPONSIBILITY

What negligence, what standing still is this?

Dante, *Purgatorio*, Canto II

One of the most impressive and inventive tools that was developed following the catastrophic failure of the international community in Rwanda was the Responsibility to Protect, the UN doctrine that establishes and maintains standards for, and supervision of, the protection of global human rights regardless of borders. It recognized that intervention is sometimes necessary to protect the lives and rights of individuals, and that the sovereignty of the individual is more important than the sovereignty of the state.

The idea that there was an overarching responsibility to protect human beings from trespasses against their bodily integrity by their own governments was fundamental to the UN Charter and the Geneva Conventions of the 1940s. But the concept of "human security" really came to the fore after the Genocide against the Tutsi in Rwanda. Canada's minster of foreign affairs at the time, Lloyd Axworthy, described it this way in 1999:

In essence, human security means safety for people from both violent and non-violent threats. It is a condition or state of being characterized by freedom from pervasive threats to people's rights, their safety, or even their lives. From a foreign policy perspective, human security is perhaps best understood as a shift in perspective or orientation. It is an alternative way of seeing the world, taking people as its point of reference, rather than focusing exclusively on the security of territory or governments. Like other security concepts— national security, economic security, food security—it is about protection. Human security entails taking preventive measures to reduce vulnerability and minimize risk, and taking remedial action where prevention fails.

The following year, the UN Peace Operations' Brahimi Report also argued for the need to protect civilians, as had the earlier Rome Statute, which called on every state to bring perpetrators of international crimes against humanity to justice and led to the establishment of the International Criminal Court. And most significantly, in 2001 Canada's International Commission on Intervention and State Sovereignty published *The Responsibility to Protect*, known colloquially as R2P.

After discussions with UN Secretary-General Kofi Annan, Lloyd Axworthy had chaired the initial advisory board on the subject and secured funding from the Government of Canada for the commission that developed it, which was co-chaired by Gareth Evans and Mohamed Sahnoun. Following four years of powerful advocacy on the part of Axworthy, Evans, and other passionate proponents such as Michael Ignatieff, Allan Rock and Paul Martin, the Responsibility to Protect doctrine was adopted by the UN General Assembly at the 2005 World Summit. This revolutionary new initiative provided the parameters for intervention: "We are prepared to take collective action . . . should peaceful means be inadequate and national authorities are manifestly failing to protect their populations from genocide, war crimes, ethnic cleansing and crimes against humanity."

R2P was radical. And because of it, for a brief, shining moment, establishment of a post–Cold War peace seemed possible. R2P rendered the basic premise of a nation-state— its sovereignty—no longer an absolute. It also imposed on all other nation-states the responsibility to go into conflict zones beyond their own borders when it was necessary to protect civilians.

The guardrails of R2P were akin to those of just war theory: the ends must justify the means, violence must be kept to the minimum required to attain the goal, and one must distinguish between combatants and non-combatants and avoid harming the latter. In similar fashion, R2P justified intervention across borders on the basis of three fundamental ideas: 1) the responsibility of every state to protect its citizens; 2) the obligation of the world community to aid a specific state in carrying out its obligation to provide security for its nationals; and 3) the obligation of the international community, in situations where a state fails to fulfill its obligation to safeguard its citizens, to take whatever steps are necessary to stop these abuses.*

But R2P was put into operation only twice. Once, successfully, in Kenya, when after years of brewing tension over ethnic favouritism, a disputed election led to hundreds of ethnic Kikuyu (including children) being slaughtered by machete. Kenya was on the brink of genocide, but Kofi Annan led a team of international mediators there; they successfully negotiated a power-sharing arrangement and social reforms, and the crisis passed.

The second time was decidedly not a success; in fact, the outcome may have been worse than the status quo. In 2011, R2P was used to justify the UN-sanctioned NATO intervention in Libya. This international military mission soon evolved from protecting the civilian population from the Gadhafi regime's use of excessive force to quell a civil insurrection to supporting regime change. As a result, unauthorized forces and militias escalated the conflict to a level of catastrophic chaos that is still ongoing, destabilizing the entire region.

With R2P, the UN had the tool and the mandate, but as with its peacekeeping efforts, it had to contract out the intervention. The UN had no strategic oversight over the military operation, nor the means to control it. The commander, Canadian three-star general Charles Bouchard, told me he'd

---

* With R2P, six criteria must be met before force is used: right authority, just cause, right intention, last resort, proportional means and reasonable prospect. The criteria provide enormous scope to diplomats, but the military face real challenges in translating them into operational plans.

never briefed the UN, just NATO. He'd expected NATO to then brief the UN, but that didn't happen. When the Gadhafi regime collapsed, Russia and China rightly condemned the mission for its abuse of the mandate, which gave these two outlier nations their much-sought-after excuse to put the kibosh on R2P altogether. Developing countries perceived it as a potential free pass for outside powers to intervene in their affairs, even invade them. The five permanent members of the Security Council and other major powers feared R2P could force them to engage in conflicts that not only were of no benefit to them, but also ran counter to their own global ambitions. Painfully, many nations decided that R2P interventions might be worse than the mass abuses they were designed to prevent.

Where R2P did succeed was in making the protection of civilians in intrastate conflicts something the United Nations needed to address. Kofi Annan went on to create his protection of civilians mandate (now called people-centred security). Concurrently, he organized an international advisory board on genocide prevention, to which he appointed, among others, Gareth Evans, Desmond Tutu and me.

To support my work on this board, I turned to the Montreal Institute for Genocide and Human Rights Studies at Concordia University. Its director, Frank Chalk, and I decided to conduct research on how to effectively implement R2P and how to address the doctrine's fundamental weakness: the political will to use it. We commenced a two-year project that culminated in 2010 with the publication of *Mobilizing the Will to Intervene*. Our report argued for a paradigm shift in what nations believe to be their self-interest. From the text: "We need to redefine our national interest more broadly, not only to help broken and failing states, but also to help and protect ourselves."

We argued that mass atrocities, genocide and conflicts in other countries have direct ramifications on our own security; for example, the rage, disease, poverty and radicalization exacerbated in displacement and refugee camps can have extreme consequences locally and even overseas, given that global diasporas can become deeply discontented when their new hosts fail to respond to catastrophes in their home countries.

Our report proved so compelling that the US National Security Council, at the urging of Samantha Power, who was serving on the council as senior director for multilateral affairs and human rights, adopted three of our recommendations and set up permanent bodies to monitor the security risks mass atrocities can create.

It was a small but important innovation: we could take advantage of national self-interest, instead of fighting it. Though stable countries may not be inclined to help failing states out of altruism, we found we could appeal to their own self-interest to provide necessary intervention and protection.

If the United Nations had had the means and the member states had had the will to bravely and nimbly implement these new ideas and new tools for peace, they could have created shifts in thought that might have taken us farther toward planetary security and peace.

Still, good people continue to push forward doggedly in search of the ways and means to secure peace and prevent another genocide, a slow and grinding effort, complicated by endless frustration—as when Russia's invasion of Ukraine showed that all the work we've done to prevent such violations can be trampled into the dust by a bully. That that invasion was allowed to happen without globally unanimous condemnation backed up by boots on the ground shows just how hollow the commitments member nations have made to the values set out in the UN Charter really are.

When making a list of our areas of negligence, from finding so many excuses to turn away as others suffer and die to countenancing the use of child soldiers, the existence of nuclear weapons is toward the top. These weapons of total and mutually assured destruction are an affront to life itself. Threats of the explosive use of nuclear weapons—whether explicitly by Russia as a tactic in the war in Ukraine, or implicitly in the ongoing readiness and posture of the United States when it comes to such weapons—bring the entire human family to the brink of extinction. By miscalculation, accident, design or madness, the unthinkable could cascade down upon humanity.

There can be no peace, no sustainable future, while these irresponsible weapons remain such a threat.

REVOLUTIONS

When for a better life thou changedst worlds
Dante, *Purgatorio,* Canto XXIII

We've arrived in our current era not through a slow
and predictable evolution, but by way of a dynamic,
unanticipated series of revolutions: social, cultural,
structural, environmental and—the most rapid and
transforming of all—information technology and communication. Even though the digital age is still in its infancy, it is
already like the air we breathe.

In the late 1990s, I held discussions with futurists about
the potentials of technology—things like artificial intelligence
and biomechanical interfacing—as I considered what skills
commanders of the next millennium would require. They
told me that by the 2020s, we would have moved beyond the
RoboCop exoskeletons military researchers were starting to
develop to biophysical interfaces far beyond eyeball scans
and touch screens—to the actual fusion of living human and
machine. They warned that the way our brains make decisions, through deductive reasoning, was simply too slow to
keep up with this integrated technology.

Today, right on schedule, the enhancement of human beings by way of genetic engineering, artificial intelligence and nano-technology is a hot topic. The movement is being called "trans-humanism," which is an interesting continuum from Dante's neologism *trasumanar*, a term he coined to describe the spiritual transformation a human being must undergo before they can ascend beyond the terrestrial paradise to the celestial. My fear with transhumanism is that the human / computer interface will prioritize the tech side, leaving the human being as only the platform the technology will function on. It is my fervent hope that military leaders will have the brain power to understand, if not answer, the philosophical and spiritual questions transhumanism raises. Are we now preparing future battalion-level and higher commanders in West Point, the Defence College or the Royal Military College for this coming era, or are they still trying to figure out PowerPoint?

Of course, these questions are not unique to the military. If we allow technology to develop unchecked, we could all be left in the dark. As just one instance, we don't have a firm handle on Google's capabilities, yet Google is already pervasive and worldwide, borderless and limitless—and ungoverned. What happens if Google goes rogue? Who is really running it? Do we even notice when its search results are skewed? Where is the information-savvy leadership to point the way forward?

Social media has become so ubiquitous, so rapidly, it has leapt beyond the control of anyone but the individuals and mega-corporations who own the platforms. These platforms and their algorithms have been associated with a global decline in political democracy and the rise of populism. As we know, the tendency of social media users to exist in a bubble with others who share similar views, opinions and content served up steadily by their platforms of choice encourages polarization and reinforces extreme views. As studies have shown, users engage more with shocking, hateful, rage-inducing posts than positive ones (aside from pictures of kittens). People who want to expand their reach on social media understand that dynamic and learn to shamelessly feed it.

Without any doubt, social media has trapped some people in online echo chambers, where they remain misguided, unfocused and unprogressive. I believe, however, that our current polarization is not a lasting state, but a sign of the immaturity of the medium. I don't claim to know where the future of technology is heading, but I do know that our leaders need to better grasp its enormous potential (both positive and negative). Being able to connect with everyone, instantaneously, has in many ways brought us closer together, but at the same time, social media can also be an isolating force we have to work to counteract.

Another major revolution we are seeing today is the countervailing force to the unleashing of negative emotions on social media. Us versus Other thinking is beginning to crumble and, in a diverse, inclusive, pluralist revolution, arbitrary classifications are being exposed as false and damaging.

There are growing pains here too. White, Western males like me were the first to enjoy the benefits of "universal" tenets protecting our rights. But human rights have been appallingly slow in "trickling down" to all; the revolution upon us now is in the full application of those rights. Individual human rights are finally beginning to be truly respected, not merely tolerated. (How I detest that word. Who are we to "tolerate" another? The "tolerance" concept really epitomizes the privilege of the old guard, who felt so "kind" to tolerate the existence of genders, races, cultures, religions, sexual orientations, or any classification other than their own.)

At the same time, paradoxically, rights have never appeared so fragile. More nations have been moving to the political right, and leadership in democratic countries is becoming more autocratic, demonstrating less and less tolerance for the demands of the enormous diversity of populations and the complexities of respecting their human rights. These hardline, near-demagogic leaders are creating significant frictions, and citizens are legitimately concerned about their ability to handle contemporary complexity.

I rejoice in the revolutionary rejection of hardline and often arbitrary classifications. Battles rage, and backlash is brutal, but over and over we are witnessing the democratization of art and ideas and the amplification of voices that have been subjugated for centuries. Once the patriarchy and supremacy have gasped their last, I can only imagine the depth of insight and wisdom that will come to the fore.

Such fundamental social changes are also provoking a structural revolution, a fissure in our faith in long-standing institutions. Changes in society created a demand for transparency and a drive to know what goes on behind the curtain—to ensure these institutions are behaving in ways that are right and just, pertinent, and up to date with fundamental human rights.

We've been ripping down the walls around every conservative institution of our society. We've dug into the churches and found abhorrent unethical behaviours. We've challenged the authority of the police. Access to information laws, no matter how foot-dragging the response, have helped us to scrutinize government, and over the years since they were enacted, reporters and researchers have dug up troubling instances of indifference, mismanagement and outright corruption.

These so-called bastions have been crumbling, and with them, so have our old reference points. For me, born in khaki and raised in the army, the most personally significant walls to challenge have been in the military. That most proudly conservative mainstay of our society never had transparency. And once we bothered to take a closer look with new eyes, we saw that the military was deeply out of step in numerous areas. We had lost touch with the fundamental, driving ideas behind our work, our world.

In the 1970s, when the Canadian government started working on the Charter of Rights and Freedoms, it ordered the Department of National Defence to pilot implementing the Charter post haste. But the military was petrified that applying the Charter to its own operations and administration would undermine its ability to control the conduct of its operations. This was an era in the Canadian Forces when secretaries (always women) were hired as much for their looks as their abilities, and homosexuality was a fireable offence. You can imagine how we handled an expanded gender perspective and LGBTQ+ inclusion in recruitment. We were so confident of our existing privileges that, to the military powers that be, equality felt like oppression.

In 1982, when the Charter of Rights and Freedoms was signed into law, the Canadian Armed Forces continued to resist its implementation within the military, spending years (and who knows how much money) fighting it in court. Though the thought clearly escaped the leadership of the day, it struck me as incredibly ironic for the brass to fight the Charter so vigorously when our servicemembers pledge to die in defence of our fundamental laws. Ultimately, in 1989, the generals simply turned to the troops and said, "We lost, so get on with it." Meaning, get on with permitting women in combat units, get on with changing the concept of privilege, and get on with creating a far more transparent organization. It was such a dismissive attitude to such an important advancement.

Though media is a crucial instrument of transparency, the military continued to treat journalists and reporters as the enemy. Prior to the 1990s, if there was a problem within our institution, we were able to get away with putting up barbed wire at the main gate of our camps and sending a young lieutenant out to say "No comment." When that was no longer an acceptable tactic, the military reluctantly began to talk, though the leadership still tried everything to avoid it. It took a long time for the Armed Forces to realize that we could not carry on being a conservative bastion in isolation; we had to help the nation move ahead, not hold it back. So, how did we adjust to this revolutionary new attitude? With lots of bumps, such as the army brass's retrenchment after the Somalia inquiry soured the general public's opinion of the forces.

What was—and still is—required is active, not passive, leadership. But there are still some who subscribe to an "If it ain't broke, don't fix it" attitude. I would argue that in this revolutionary new era, maintaining the status quo is not holding the line, but actively regressing.

This leads me to reconsider the entire notion of the use of force as a component to establishing peace and security in the world. I do believe that the threat of the use of force can be a strong prod to move us *beyond* the use of force, even to never having to use it; security forces have been able to prevent conflicts by their mere presence. The warrior ethic remains the fundamental raison d'être of the military, but it's essential that use of force is not our only tool. Being a master of one siloed discipline is no longer adequate in an era requiring complex, integrated solutions. Fundamentally, generals who only know how to fight have outlived their usefulness. Knowing how to command troops in operational theatres is only the baseline for soldiering in our era. The skills and knowledge these complex times demand go way beyond that.

Obviously, the most far-reaching existential revolution we are currently facing is human-caused climate change.

To my father's generation, environmental resources seemed limitless and the stability of our planet absolute. There was oil, fish, wood and land in abundance and, so too, possibility and potential. Given that they had no sense that there were limits on Mother Earth, it's hard to blame them for reaping what seemed so generously provided.

My generation, the so-called baby boomers, are the ones who should be held accountable when future generations are walking around in oxygen masks. We were the first to realize the impact of human activity on the environment, and yet we continued to take and take. Mine was the first generation to grow up with the image before our eyes of our magnificent little blue-green ball in the middle of the vast universe. When the first astronauts sent back pictures of the Earth from space, we were forced to face our planet's fragility and, in the same glance, we were also granted a vision that humanity might find a way to commune together as one. I can't overstate the profound impact these images had on us, which makes it even more appalling that we failed to act. It was perfectly clear that we had to protect the Earth to ensure our own survival, but even from that self-centred starting point, my generation failed to recognize the need for a communion with the environment and other people that would sustain both us and our planet into the future.

Oh, we talked about it. We held summits. We marched. We slapped on bumper stickers reading "Save the Whales." And while we have been mulling tactics—Should we use solar energy instead of natural gas? give up meat? buy an electric car?—the real question is whether humanity will continue to exist at all.

I am beyond proud of today's youth climate activists. They seem to have been propelled by necessity to be exponentially stronger, smarter and more *perspicace* than my generation. They are brave and intransigent, and they need to be. It has taken us, steeped in our Western materialist mindset, three generations to realize that unless there is a communion between ourselves and the planet, we will never be able to thrive. Instead, we will be in perpetual survival mode, each and all suffering the consequences of our reckless choices and our ignorance.

Environmental disasters, which have been on the rise in number and severity, will not only affect our ecology, they will also have real security consequences. Events induced by climate change—flooding, drought, hurricanes, forest fires—exacerbate resource scarcity, creating increased competition for water, land and food that leads to conflict between and within nations. The displacement of people due to weather catastrophes is already creating tensions and conflicts between host countries and displaced communities.

Climate change will continue to exacerbate existing political and social tensions, particularly in areas with weak governance and political instability. Even in the most stable nations on Earth, frictions around fundamental resources are brewing. When I served in the Senate of Canada, we senators debated signing the 2010 UN resolution recognizing "the right to safe and clean drinking water" as an essential human right. Canada holds almost a quarter of the world's renewable fresh water, and yet the Conservative government of the time refused to sign the resolution because it would obligate us to give water to the Americans if they continued to suffer drought and their demands on the resource (from growing food to building golf courses in the desert) continued to increase. These parliamentarians wanted us to keep the door open to selling our water instead.

I considered this a gross perversion—that we who hold this life-giving resource would wish to profit from it. Not only was this attitude morally flawed, but it was also absurd from a defence perspective. If the US ever wanted our water, they would use all means to simply take it.

Climate change should be the common enemy that brings us together, but it doesn't affect all of us equally, at least not yet. But we have in fact moved on from climate change to climate crisis. As such, our goal must be to think strategically and long term, as well as ethically and with a shared perspective on managing global assets; the environmental revolution is a global one, whether we all choose to acknowledge it or not.

Many of us who were alive in the late twentieth century hoped that the new millennium would usher in another period of enlightenment—the Millennium of Humanity. But the first two decades of the 2000s, punctuated at the start by 9/11, have been full of regressions.

I spent a year at Harvard doing research on child soldiers soon after the Twin Towers came down. I saw first-hand a world power that had been hit in its soul. Pearl Harbor shook the United States back in 1941, but the attack was in Hawaii— far enough from the mainland for many Americans to feel a disconnect. In 2001, however, they were attacked at "home," and the impact on the American psyche was—and continues to be—massive.

Then came the war on terror, the wars in Afghanistan and Iraq, the government clampdowns after the hope-filled days of the Arab Spring, the annihilation of Syria, refugee crises, grotesque populism in the forms of Donald Trump and Victor Orbán, and a host of other regressions of the most serious kind. Current isolationist movements are not initiating anything new, they are reacting. As the futurist Peter Leyden wrote, "Trump is a symptom of something much bigger and more fundamental going on in the world. So are the people behind Brexit in Great Britain. They are not driving the change, they are reacting to the change. They are not showing the way forward, they are making desperate attempts to cling to the past, a past that is gone forever."

I believe this is a painful pendulum swing, driven by power-grabbing leaders appealing to those who long for the "good old days" (of systemic inequality)—ruthless, unprincipled individuals who see an opportunity to make both a buck and a name for themselves by proposing ridiculously simple solutions to non-existent issues. These huckster politicians aim to keep the level of debate low and confined to issues on the fringes, because that is so much easier than delving into the complexity of the existential problems we're facing. (Such a different political scenario than the 1960s, when Canada proposed universal health care and old age pensions and debated the issues intelligently, leading to significant beneficial social change; and when protests and legal challenges ended segregation in the United States.)

So, what are our solutions for the future? Build a wall? Merely survive? Or should our aim in all areas—peace and security, the environment, personal well-being—be to prevent problems before they become critical and assuage the anger that exacerbates them?

First and foremost, we have to agree this is what we want. I agree with my whole heart. Do you?

With that goal established, we need to consider our strategy. Seventy-five years ago, the United Nations was formed to work for peace after years of world war. But throughout its history, as I've already discussed, the UN's *pacifique* ideals haven't always translated into security for the planet's most vulnerable inhabitants. Far from it. Too often, peace has become an option only after blood was shed. With each new crisis, the UN and its member states continually play catch-up, focusing their efforts on resolving existing conflicts. Whether it's peacebuilding, crisis response or post-conflict reconciliation, each of these phases comes too late to really achieve peace. We've created valuable conflict resolution tools, but they are entirely reactive. A conflict has to turn into a crisis before these tools are even considered, let alone deployed. And then the effort to sustain them falters.

We—as countries and as human beings—can choose to come together and assist others, or to isolate ourselves and ignore everyone else. We can choose to adhere to laws, conventions and rules, or we can choose to bend and break them.

It is our choice. We can choose to shape the future, or just survive what is thrown at us. We can choose to prevent conflict, protect civilians and preserve our Earth. We can choose to embrace the exciting revolutions of our era and pull ourselves up and off the mountain of purgatory, or risk regressing to those old circles of hell.

RENAISSANCE

He mastered all; and let the idiots talk

Dante, *Purgatorio*, Canto XXVI

have always been taken with the idea of the Renaissance Man, someone (of any gender) with a mastery of many different disciplines: artist, philosopher, mathematician, militarist, humanist. The Italian Renaissance was a period of unified and unifying change that reached across disciplines. From the unprecedented genius of Leonardo da Vinci to the very concept of humanism (which first prioritized individual human beings), the Renaissance sparked a revolution in values and a new way of interpreting and defining the world and the human condition. This profoundly unifying moment signalled a revolutionary emotional and philosophical shift from the past and pointed the way to other important revolutions (scientific, industrial). It was also the starting point from which modern ideas of individualism and statecraft sprang.

Dante Alighieri wrote his *Divine Comedy* at the tail end of the Dark Ages. That era was defined by economic and cultural stagnation under the almost total power and influence of the Catholic Church. Religion imposed overwhelming limits on freedom of thought and of action throughout the

Middle Ages, until the fourteenth century, when revolutions across disciplines brought Europe from the small-minded Dark Ages into the glorious Renaissance.

Nowhere is this more apparent than in the fine art of the period—Leonardo's *The Last Supper* and *Mona Lisa*, Michelangelo's Sistine Chapel and statue of David—in which artists achieved a change of perspective, both literal and figurative. Literally, the first use of perspective to show the relationship between objects created a depth never before seen in paint or stone. And figuratively, these artists and thinkers altered their entire perspective on the universe and their own place in it, centring it more on the human than the divine.

Many decades of crisis and reaction lit the spark of the Renaissance. After the collapse of the Holy Roman Empire, there was no single power other than the Catholic Church to ensure order, and so societies became localized. (Compare this with the end of the bipolarity of the Cold War.) The use of diplomacy, including the deployment of resident ambassadors, was developed during the Renaissance, and the Treaty of Lodi created a period of peace and stability in Italy (much like the United Nations attempted to do worldwide, five hundred years later).

Trade in luxury goods brought money to the cities, creating a class of citizens who wanted to rearrange society to meet their new circumstances. The Medici family, for example, funded and commissioned art, spawning an unparalleled period of creative innovation (like the Gates Foundation supporting humanitarian aid today, or the new interest of billionaires in space travel). New wealth put pressure on old ideas, and this caused a disjunction between the ruling nobility and the newly powerful merchants. (I see a similar disjunction today between the 1 percent and the rest of society.)

New technologies such as the printing press (like the internet today) were democratizing access to information, bringing ideas beyond the educated elite to a wider world. Advances in shipbuilding (think aviation and aerospace engineering) allowed the crossing of oceans and a realization of the scale of the world. Technology was also changing the way war was fought, with the medieval knight being supplanted by soldiers with guns and cannons (similar to how the nuclear bomb changed distance warfare).

These few examples illustrate how—then and now—old tools no longer work in the new normal.

What change will our revolutionary times invite? For me, the guiding lessons from the Renaissance are that peace cannot be achieved when there is a wolf at the door. That learning across disciplines, and the sharing of information and ideas, is critical to finding productive and sophisticated solutions to complex problems. And that putting the human being—and the planet that sustains us—at the forefront of decision-making is essential. The Renaissance introduced the era of humanism, in part as a result of the bubonic plague, which killed so many people the old order could no longer sustain itself, and also in part as a result of a period of peace, which diverted creativity toward art, music, diplomacy and philosophy.

We've had our global plague and, despite how dire the present moment can feel, we are slowly reducing the number and length of conflicts around the world. Is it possible that we might soon turn our attention away from ego-driven competition for wealth, power and status long enough to make space for new ideas that will help us survive the changes coming at us?

Peace cannot be found through power; it is not an advantage gained by force. Peace requires a catalyst, a unifying ideology.

Unless one is deliberately divorcing oneself from the rest of humanity, our interconnectedness is impossible to ignore. But we will require more than the tools and equipment that technology provides to foster our connections. Like the Florentines during the Renaissance, we require a deeper change at our core, a fundamental shift in perspective.

Humanism was the Renaissance period's guiding principle, informing all disciplines and aspects of life. What will be our guiding, unifying principle going forward?

GIUBUNTU

This is in mortal hearts the motive power
This binds together and unites the earth.

Dante, *Paradiso,* Canto i

H umanism defined the Renaissance, eradicated the old
order and transformed art, politics and religion. But it
also led, like an arrow's flight, to an individualism that
became the cornerstone of industrialization, capitalism
and colonialism. In our era of revolutions, nothing is clearer
than the need for us to reconnect to each other, in all our
humanity, and to the Earth.

We are at the point of such existential risk that we need to
abandon self-interest. That era has failed all but the 1 percent,
and they are failing the rest of us every day. Our nuances and
differences can be, and need to be, respected and celebrated.
But to thrive we must move forward without friction and
competition. This is a level of unity I believe we haven't even
perceived yet, but it is the only thing that will permit us to
reinforce our *ensemble*, find the positives in our differences,
and prevent conflict before it happens.

Peace, as we have known it since the end of the last world
war, hasn't been peace at all, because we have never broken

the cycle of truces and conflicts fed by separation, inequality and isolation. To use myself again as an example, two hundred years after the British won the battle for what became Canada on the Plains of Abraham, my father told me I'd never get promoted because I had a French-Canadian name. Fifty years later, as a general and Canadian senator, I asked my government how we should commemorate that significant moment in our history and the sacrifices made on all sides on those plains; I was told that we didn't want to open that can of worms, because it would just generate more argument and debate. Soon after, I was riding in a car with the future prime minister, who told me his father (Prime Minister Pierre Elliott Trudeau) told him we would *never* be able to satisfy the most extreme French separatist elements in Quebec. Clearly, Canada is not at peace. We are still living in a temporary state of truce after more than 250 years!

Tutsi and Hutu, Ukraine and Russia, Israel and Palestine, Han Chinese and Uyghur: grievances that began decades or centuries ago keep us in perpetual purgatory. Sooner rather than later, human-caused climate change will require us to come together against a common adversary, and we will need to figure out how to reshape our relationship with each other and with our planet. We have to abandon the cynical view that we're each in this life for ourselves alone.

Cultures with long enough histories all seem to create words to describe oneness among humans—the ties that bind us to each other and the planet. The national motto of Rwanda includes the Kinyarwanda word *ubumwe*, which means "unity" (*umoja* in Swahili). The Celtic word *céile* can refer to husband and wife, or an enemy in battle, both instances of people bound to each other. 五伦 (or *wǔ lún* in Mandarin pinyin) refers to fundamental relationships in society, while *asabiyyah* is an Arabic concept of solidarity and cohesion in society, co-operation for the public good. German *Mensch* means "human being," which in Yiddish gained the specifically positive characteristics of ethical integrity and moral rightness.

The Zulu word *ubuntu* grew from the phrase *umuntu ngumuntu ngabantu* ("a person is a person because of other people"). Justice Yvonne Mokgoro of South Africa describes *ubuntu* as encompassing "group solidarity, compassion, respect, human dignity, conformity to basic norms and collective unity; in its fundamental sense it denotes humanity and morality." A Black constitutional lawyer and apartheid-era activist, Mokgoro explains that the spirit of *ubuntu* "emphasizes respect for human dignity, marking a shift from confrontation to conciliation."

Most First Nations' languages have a word or phrase that expresses the interconnectedness of all things as "We are all related." Métis professor Paul L.A.H. Chartrand from the University of Saskatchewan explains that, in Cree, *Niw_hk_m_ kanak* ("All my relations") encompasses all humans, including those who have passed on and those who are yet to be born, as well as plants, animals, and the Earth itself. Ojibwe linguist James Vukelich Kaagegaabaw explains that the word *giidinawendamen* ("we are all related") is also inclusive ("we" referring to all people, as opposed to "we" as distinct from you, which employs a different pronoun marker). "In a spiritual sense," he says, "you are addressing the entire universe as relatives."

Sometimes new ideas require new words that can't be captured by a single language. When lawyer Raphael Lemkin tried to find a word to describe the enormity of the Holocaust, he took *geno* from the Greek for "tribe" or "race" and *cide* from the Latin for "killing" to form the word *genocide*—the intentional destruction of an ethnic or religious group—and then spent months advocating for its use by the United Nations.

I believe it's time for us to find an all-embracing word with meaningful and positive roots to express the conceptual framework by which we, as inhabitants of this planet, will join together, in communion and coexistence with our environment, to make the leap away from our current path to self-destruction.

I love the symbolism of a web; it is interconnected but also localized; it can grow wider and deeper to handle diverse input; it's natural and ubiquitous. While webs are made by thousands of different species of spider, they all adhere to fundamental building principles. Charmingly, *utando*—Swahili for "cobweb"—looks remarkably similar to *uthando*—Zulu for "love"—and *unity* in English, as well as the beautiful concept *ubuntu*. But of course, the word *web* is now inextricably associated with the internet, so to use it in any other context would create confusion.

If we were to build a new word to express what is required to move us forward, just as Dante coined the word *trasumanar* ("beyond human") to express his ascent to *Paradiso*, we could pair the *gi* from the Ojibwe *giidinawendamen* (*gi* also being a Greek word for Earth) with *ubuntu*. This could perhaps capture the idea of our unified Team Earth lodestar.

Giubuntu.

For twenty-five years I struggled my way out of hell and slogged through purgatory, isolated and alone, viewing the world from the perspective of a warrior. Assessing risk, watching my six, locked in struggle, seeking victory. Trying desperately to solve the world's problems with the tools, the language and the ethos of combat.

There was comfort in the familiarity of my struggle, so I continued my punishing self-imposed mission to atone for humanity's failures, and my own. But when the doctors told me I was working myself to an early grave, and I allowed that to sink in, I realized that the cyclical state of purgatory I was living in was no longer sustainable.

In Dante's allegory, he does not pass easily into the spheres of heaven. First, he must step through a wall of fire. When I faced my own metaphorical wall of fire—that is, my mortality—I at last understood that the warrior in me had to give way to the human. And I knew I could seek, find and accept peace in my soul.

I wish I could explain this change better. I am a long way from having the gifts of expression of a poet such as Dante, but like Dante, who states at the beginning of *Paradiso* that he passes on his poem to the world with the hope that "better voices after me" will reveal more of the truth, I wish for the same. All I can say is that after I was forced to the edge of the

Earth, my path upward was suddenly clear. As a result, the aim of this book, which I had initially hoped would provide a prescription for peace, has become more humble and more personal.

In Part Three I try to outline the new construct of my soul, the new me, by describing the interconnected constellation of lodestars I am following as I reconnect with and rebuild my own humanity. A leadership philosophy grounded in *bienveillance*. A focus on conflict prevention designed to anticipate and shape a future grounded in security and serenity. Informed by diverse, integrated knowledge. With a culturally nuanced lexicon. Just and fair. *Sans frontières*. The Peace.

And, perhaps, my modest personal epiphanies can help create a path for you too.

PART THREE

PEACE

This way goes he who goeth after peace

Dante, *Purgatorio*, Canto XXIV

I used to see my way as a warrior through the sight of a gun. Firearms use gyroscopes to maintain stabilization regardless of outside influence—a mechanical system of rapidly spinning disks around a fixed axis that keeps the direction constant. What a perfect metaphor for the purgatory of the old guard, the old me. A lethal weapon aiming for peace by staying steadfast at the axis of cyclical patterns of motion, with only a hope and a prayer that it won't need to be fired.

In contrast, Dante describes his paradise as a solar system. The planets, free from the flawed Earth, together create a holistic, organic system of consistent, interdependent movement, each sphere separate but never isolated, revolving but still yielding stability. Little did the poet know (though perhaps he imagined), our solar system is now understood to be even more dynamic and magnificent, with the planets not only orbiting within space but also through it, projecting into the ever-expanding universe.

After I confronted my wall of fire, I vowed that my journey would no longer be guided by my old means; I would abandon the narrow, the rigid, the reactive, the defensive.

I believe that humanity is on the precipice of a major leap forward, but we have so far been too afraid or apathetic to cast off the status quo. The situation is increasingly urgent. Our problems—climate disasters, plagues, wars—are truly global: no one is immune. The impacts of our nascent Cybercene, and our overarching Anthropocene, are borderless. Despite the seductive rhetoric of so-called populists, there is no such thing as "them" and "us." We are all "us." Attempting to retrench and defend our local interests, our territory, against "the other" is a vain and self-destructive exercise.

All of us on this planet will face the future together, and to do so effectively we require a new conceptual framework. One that will address the root causes of problems, so we can anticipate and prevent them. One that will connect us not only with each other but with our planet. One that will bring us to a state of peace and security, free from fear, want and indignity, so that we can fulfill our human potential rather than merely survive. One that will sustain our drive toward a future that is well beyond what we can imagine from where we are now.

Our present condition is so vulnerable to destruction that we live in constant anxiety and instability. To thrive—actually, to even survive the challenges facing us—we need to move to a place where human security is a given, where we are safe from violence, where our basic needs are satisfied and our future is sustainable.

I know the dangers of ad hominem arguments, but I find hope in my own recent transformation. At a moment of extreme vulnerability, love came to me like an apparition. I had never experienced it before, not as a child, nor as an adult. (I was so rarely with my children when they were young, I missed the golden opportunities they offered me. Over recent years, though, love has opened me up to love and our relationships have at last blossomed.) To avoid falling into despair, I'd spent decades rushing in circles, attempting to fix everything I could fix. With love came a more radical thought: perhaps I could allow myself to discover a renewed enthusiasm for existence, even a state of peace.

My love and I married and moved into a house that had already survived centuries, surrounded by trees, rivers, mountains and farmland. Here I felt close to the rhythm of the seasons (a stark contrast to my previous standard environment of computer screens and airports). We have created a home in that house, which has given me the security, at last, to function day to day without constant anxiety and struggle. This *prise de conscience* allowed me to consider what our world might look like beyond the absence of war. This is a work in progress, a path I am still exploring and one I can't travel alone.

Dante lived at the start of a period of invention so great it gave birth to an entirely new perspective on humanity and the individual human being, breaking (or at least cracking) the glass ceiling of religion. Today, we are experiencing the extension of that humanist perspective in extraordinary advances for long-marginalized groups demanding systemic change.

Of course, speaking out against the status quo always has a cost, in sweat and tears, even blood. Copernicus (another Renaissance polymath) was sentenced to life under house arrest because he stated that the Earth was not the centre of the universe. Today we're witnessing the birth of profound revolutionary ideas at the same time as we're experiencing significant social, political and philosophical regressions, accompanied by threats and abuse of power. I believe—I hope—these are the last desperate gasps of a self-interested old guard attempting to retain their unjustified power over others. The rise of populist authoritarianism in reaction to rightful insistence on truth, freedom, equality and women's empowerment is just the patriarchy pushing back against its long overdue demise.

This hope of mine springs from two sources. One is the decades of shame and guilt I have suffered for failing the people of Rwanda in the genocide. I have long felt that it is my personal responsibility to prevent the genocide from being forgotten, to push for reforms and keep moving yardsticks. It's hard to capture in words the perspective this has given me, because it may seem paradoxical. The best I've heard it expressed is by a nun who had walked the hills of Rwanda during the genocide with bags of money, attempting to buy back the lives of her postulant and novice sisters from the Hutu *génocidaires*. Sister Marie Joseph wrote to me to say that because I had descended into the belly of the beast, lived in the thick of the most depraved and abhorrent hell on Earth, bore the burden of command in such a horrific time, and managed to come out the other side, I possessed a privileged understanding of how to love and help humanity, and that would be my mission.

The other source of my hope is my certainty. I truly believe that humanity is going to achieve a state of communion with the planet and freedom from conflict and strife, even if it takes a couple of centuries. If I can find peace, anyone— maybe everyone—can. And once we do find it, we will gain the mental and emotional space to expand our capabilities and discover our unlimited possibilities and purpose in the universe. Oh, how I'd love to be around for that!

As I understand the Darwinian concept of evolution, it posits that the strongest—those who continuously fight to be the "best"—keep us going. Such an understanding inculcates a constant combative sensibility that drives us to fight our own. I refuse to believe this driven vision is the essence and calling of human beings, that we lead lives that are "nasty, brutish, and short." I believe our spirit, the deeper being within us, can push us beyond survival by way of beating the shit out of each other, to thriving in symbiosis with the universe around us.

I just hope that humanity won't need to self-destruct, like I almost did, to learn these lessons. Perhaps climate change— the biggest threat to our existence—will be our great unifier, given that everyone will have to get on board for the whole of us to survive. Or perhaps we'll find a much more positive catalyst.

Naysayers will call my optimism naive, insisting that human nature *is* barbaric and selfish. However, I am confident we can break the limitations that we create by staying locked in our egocentric, exclusionary vices.

Dante makes clear that there are always lessons to be learned, even in heaven. *Paradiso*, like Peace, is not a static end state; it is a journey of constant practice and discovery. In *Paradiso*, after the poet passes through the wall of fire, he must immerse himself in the river of forgetfulness to erase the erroneous knowledge and bad education he had received. He wades next through the river of remembrance, where he gathers whatever positive wisdom he may have learned. Only then does he ascend the spheres of heaven. Along the way, he meets people who are trying and failing to climb, who have broken promises they meant to keep, who did good deeds but in pursuit of fame and glory. And he also meets those who inspire and exemplify the virtues: courageous warriors, kings who rule with justice and value societal diversity, saints who deplore corruption, and characters who comprehend the complexities of attaining and maintaining peace.

His is a journey not of perfection, but of potential.

Like Dante's character, after my moment of truth I retained a little bit of wisdom from my past and finally cast off the stranglehold of my failings, my moral scars and, I hope, the last tentacles of status quo thinking. My journey is no longer focused, as it once was, on finding tactical answers to the problems of today, but on attempting to strategize, even shape, the future.

To light my way forward, I aim toward the lodestars of ethos, leadership, prevention, security, integration, lexicon, *sans frontières,* justice and The Peace. I hope that describing some of the steps I'm taking to reach them will also provide some illumination for your path.

ETHOS

Together, at once, with one accord

Dante, *Paradiso*, Canto XII

The military aims to inculcate a warrior ethos in all its members from the moment they don a uniform. Adopting this ethos is essential to handling the sacrifice—often the supreme sacrifice—soldiers are asked to make: to lay down their lives if that is what the mission requires. To fulfill the demands of that warrior ethos, you need not just a willingness to pick up a weapon and engage in combat, but also courage, discipline and loyalty.

This was the ethos by which I was raised and to which I once devoted my life. I know first-hand it is not only possible to adopt an ethos, it makes life easier; decisions become clearer, hardships are more bearable, and joys are more meaningful. An ethos provides a raison d'être.

Abandoning my long-held warrior ethos seemed impossible. But as Dante explains, when making transformational change one needs to bathe in the river of forgetfulness, as well as the river of remembrance. So I washed away what was unhelpful, defensive and combative, but did my best to retain the knowledge that helped me to adhere to a new ethos that was just as powerful and *more* sustaining. An ethos of peace.

It happened that just as I was moving away from my old warrior ethos, I found myself involved in the work of an international commission called Principles for Peace (P4P) that sought input on how to achieve peace from tens of thousands of stakeholders—youth, civil organizations, NGOs, governments, militaries, non-state actors and all manner of grassroots activists, as well as high-level changemakers from every region of the world. In 2022, after two years of consultations, our commission released a *Peacemaking Covenant*, which lays out the necessary shifts in approach to peacemaking, the philosophy behind them, and the overarching principles that create a framework for action: dignity, solidarity, humility, accountable security, legitimacy, integrated solutions, pluralism and subsidiarity (a five-dollar word that just means that problems should be solved as locally as possible and as globally as necessary). Spending so much time and energy considering these principles did enhance my understanding of the issues, but they weren't quite what I was seeking. As meaningful as these principles are, they were developed to serve the challenges of the day, while I had trained my eye much farther into the future.

In our complex world of extremes, my new perspective was quite simple, and not that much different from what I had been striving for in my life as a warrior: a commitment to humanity. I return to the concept of *Giubuntu*—all of humanity and the planet, in solidarity. All on the same team. Not a team of soldiers in uniforms, nor a team of nationalists waving flags, but Team Human. Team Earth. Team Life. In the military we wear uniforms to indicate belonging and cohesion, because cohesion multiplies the strength of the team, melding everyone into a unit. But cohesion in that context requires an opponent. With a *Giubuntu* ethos, we are a team with a single side. Driven by empathy instead of ego. Attempting to enable, not impose. Engaging in action to support and enhance, not to dominate for personal gain.

During my mission in Rwanda, I often stopped in villages and sat with elders. We rarely talked after our initial greeting. We just sat under a tree, present together amid the chaos. This is the communal connection I wish for all of humanity, the feeling that we are linked to each other and the planet purely by our existence. Not to give. Not to take. Just to be.

My own society has turned away from spirituality toward materialism, but many people from different cultures around the world still pay more attention to the spirit than to possessions. I am Catholic, but religion is not what I mean by spirituality. I also don't mean a state of subservience to a higher authority. Spirituality, in my view, is simply the acknowledgement of the spirit in us all, the essence of the self, imbued with self-respect and respect for others. Some people call this the soul or human consciousness, but whatever it's called, it is the source of the peace ethos I now do my best to live by.

While today, the term *humanism* is closely associated with secularism, the humanism of the fourteenth century was less a turning away from spirituality than a pivot toward celebrating the moral, cultural and civic achievements of human beings. For me, the legacy of those Renaissance humanists is our ever-increasing respect for humanity and the fundamental equality of individual human beings. They were the forebears of the modern Universal Declaration of Human Rights. Regardless of (but not in rejection of) religious beliefs, the declaration's authors and signatories intended for these rights to be respected universally, but they haven't been. That's a gap, a lapse, a danger that adopting an ethos of Peace would redress.

I struggled for decades to make the intellectual and visceral leap toward this new ethos, and I expect it would take a couple of centuries or more if humanity were to embrace such a change in perspective. When I'm asked about how I am able to take such a long view, given the suffering all around us, I can only offer the fact that the Renaissance, too, unfolded over centuries. Looking back, that seems a relatively short time to accomplish such a major shift.

I also look to the trees around my house, which are hundreds of years old. I see them as signs of the continuum of all living things, especially the indomitable human spirit, with seeds ever sprouting, roots incredibly deep, limbs always reaching toward our star, their canopies meeting but never overlapping so they won't interfere with one another, a creative force of environmental sustenance (literally, the air we breathe) as well as of astonishing beauty. In them, I strive to see myself, and all of humanity.

LEADERSHIP

With voice and gesture of a perfect leader
She recommenced . . . "Light intellectual replete with love,
Love of true good."

Dante, Paradiso, Canto xxx

Throughout my years of active service, I was taught that leadership was about achieving military success. Its bedrock was a rigid, paternalistic hierarchy; respect for the chain of command was considered essential to officers being able to carry the responsibility for the split-second life-and-death decisions that soldiers were called to make. In the hierarchies of business and government, and even in the family, the military model was often imitated as the best way to "get things done," "no questions asked."

In the military I knew, there was no tolerance for difference. (Think of the 1962 Canadian Forces Administrative Order 19-20: "Sexual Deviation: Investigation, Medical Investigation, and Disposal," informally known as the Gay Purge; not repealed until the 1990s.) There was no appetite for independent thinking. The military was averse to higher education, even among the officer corps. In fact, service members who were better educated were basically shunned, because the brass respected hands-on experience over intellect.

Though I rose to the rank of general in this milieu, I like to think that my own leadership style was always encouraging and congenial. But I know I was also demanding. I felt driven to face the issues and situations we encountered with the urgency they deserved. I still believe that those who take on positions of leadership, inside or outside the military, have a responsibility to commit themselves with vigour and rigour. But we need to do it in such a way that we don't burn out, as I did, over and over.

My wife, Marie, worked for twenty-five years running the Military Family Resource Centre at Canadian Forces Base Valcartier. She judged her efforts by the standards of the military old boys' club, demanding an extreme work ethic from herself and her staff. She accomplished extraordinary feats and earned the highest accolades, but in 2014 she crashed. She doesn't mind my sharing here that the pressure (a lot of it self-imposed) of high-intensity work in a rigidly hierarchical, male environment pushed her into a terrible emotional break- down and depression. That was around the time we found each other, both of us in a place of extreme vulnerability— she struggling with the limits of her professional persona, and me teetering on the brink of mortality, desperately reach- ing for an understanding of how to change.

As part of her recovery, Marie began researching the topic of leadership. She quickly struck on the concept of leaders who aim for *bienveillance*, rather than constantly reinforcing their own position at the top of the heap. She was done with overlords and underlings and the damage that dynamic does. Over the months that she was building herself back up, she also developed a philosophy of this new style of leadership.

The French word *bienveillance* is far more meaningful than its usual English translation, "benevolence." Literally, it means "good watching-over." *Bienveillant* leaders are as conscious of caring as they are of leading. They put human beings at the forefront of their efforts and acknowledge their own humanity. They embrace what have traditionally been considered more feminine qualities: nurturing; open, honest and reciprocal communication; and holistic solutions drawn from broad participation, as opposed to a single person calling the shots.

It was by watching and listening to Marie as she worked her way through these ideas that I came to recognize the failings of the military philosophy of command: combat-focused, macho, putting the mission before the human being, always urgent, always anticipating worst-case extremes. "Chain of command" suddenly sounded pejorative to me, suggesting the subjugation of a beast of burden. Similarly, the term "human resources" made me deeply uncomfortable; it felt like we were putting human beings in the same category as trucks and office supplies. Human beings are so much more than a resource to be deployed and organized for efficient results. Leaders need to see people in terms of their human potential. By that I mean not just the quality of what an employee produces on the job, but the whole of the complex individual, whether they are a clerk, a soldier or a self-driven workhorse like me.

Instead of focusing on profit, or perfection, or productivity—treating people as tireless and emotionless machines—

Leadership Bienveillant meets the needs of the individual, but also acts as a force multiplier. By accepting and even encouraging the natural fluctuations and diverse abilities of individuals, leaders gain access to their creativity, are rewarded by their trust, and can draw on all the other nimble qualities that help us react to complex scenarios. Even in crisis situations, an individual whose humanity—in all its vulnerability and sensitivity—is recognized, appreciated and accepted, will be willing to commit more fully to the mission, because they appreciate being recognized for who they are: a part of the solution.

Hierarchical leadership delivers a false promise of certainty, playing on our fears of the unknown and our anxiety about a changing world. But all it offers is a dead end. The leaders who can meet the challenges of the future will be inclusive, flexible and collaborative, whether at the peace table or the dinner table.

PREVENTION

Because thy life into the future reaches

Dante, *Paradiso*, Canto XVII

The Genocide against the Tutsi in Rwanda was so horrific, so extreme and so scarring, it forever altered my perspective of warfighting and peacemaking. The suffering I witnessed was more than human beings were meant to bear; it felt to me like the stuff of nightmares, of cautionary tales, rather than real life. In its wake, the warrior in me realized that the true attainment of peace is not "victory," but the prevention of violence in the first place. Anticipating crises, solving root problems, getting ahead of conflicts, and shaping the future is the only long-term mindset that leads us out of purgatory.

Prevention has been the conceptual lodestar guiding my work for the past three decades. It is the core of my international child soldier initiative, which has found its shape in the Dallaire Institute for Children, Peace and Security at Dalhousie University. Our mission is to end the use of children in armed conflict, making it *unthinkable*. We do so by focusing on preventing recruitment, instead of on picking up the pieces after children have already been abducted and abused. In this way we are attempting to break generational cycles of trauma and violence. We work with militaries, police, governments, civil society groups (especially women's groups) and even non-state actors (such as rebel fighters who are not affiliated with a government) to keep children out of the fight.

Many of the members of these groups were recruited as youngsters themselves, which is why prevention is so important as a long-term solution. Until she participated in Dallaire Institute training, one lieutenant-colonel in the People's Defence Forces in South Sudan had accepted child soldiers as a given—she had been recruited herself, with her parents' consent, when she was only seven. Reflecting on her early childhood, she told my researcher, "We were taught to kill. Nothing else. We grew up with these bad things in our mind."

When she was a child in the 1990s, her community did not protect the young from conflict; in fact, adults often encouraged children to join armed groups and become community protectors. When (or if) they returned home, they were received as heroes. (This is often the case even today, although in many communities the exact opposite can also be true. Returning child soldiers are often greeted with suspicion, and even violence, as retribution for their actions.)

The lieutenant-colonel acknowledged that her community members had not realized they were violating their children's rights. "In those days, children were being recruited to fight a cause. The cause of liberation of South Sudan," she explained. "But now we have our own country. What is happening now is just a conflict that is killing our children. To make this stop, the children must be protected, they need support and education. So I want to encourage women to take their children to school, and not allow their children to be recruited ever again."

As a soldier and a mother, she made a powerful pledge: "Today, as an enlightened person and an instructor and high-ranking officer in the SSPDF, I will never allow any child to be recruited and used in any armed forces or groups in any capacity."

Addressing issues at their root, so that violence can be prevented, is the key to any long-sighted perspective on peace. And though I promised that this part of the book would be about my personal journey, I can't help but make the case here that prevention is also a prudent global ambition to pursue.

It's a strategy that works in the case of conflict, it works in the case of disease, and most obviously and pressingly, it would work when it comes to climate change. In continuing to try to meet, even surpass, the current levels of consumption, while making the odd tweak like carbon offsetting or wishful recycling, we are seeing with the eyes of today, instead of those of the future.

Prevention is about more than keeping something from happening; it involves acting and empowering others to act. In 2005 I was sent into the Darfur region of Sudan by Paul Martin, then the Canadian prime minister, to assess our engagement in a comprehensive peace agreement meant to stop the killing of the African, non-Arab, Sudanese residents of Darfur and return people to their homes and their customary way of life. The genocide against the Darfuri has been going on since 2003;

there was no end in sight then, and there still isn't. Despite the Sudanese government's history of counterinsurgencies and mass atrocities throughout the late twentieth century, the international community never held it accountable for its misdeeds in the region. The UN and the international media's disregard—much as it had in Rwanda—emboldened the Sudanese government in Khartoum to unleash a militia, the Janjaweed, against Darfur's non-Arab population.

Prevention requires three things: identifying early warning signs of friction, preparing the necessary tools (such as the Responsibility to Protect doctrine), and—the hardest to coalesce—sparking the political will to intervene.

Conflict, like disease and environmental disaster, eventually forces decision-making, but those with resolve and foresight can head problems off *before* they go catastrophic. The lodestar when it comes to prevention is to change the mindsets of decision makers over time so that they learn to prioritize addressing root causes, patterns of injustice, systemic inequalities and historic tinderboxes that, when left to fester, become the source of rage and violence—to actually prevent predictable suffering before it happens. As UN Secretary-General António Guterres stated in 2023, "Prevention must be not only a priority, but *the* priority of everything we do. That means we need a huge cultural change to affirm the centrality of prevention."

Shifting gears back to how the prevention lodestar has affected my own work and life, I am finally, after decades of pinballing among overwhelming and draining demands, trying to become responsible to myself and those around me by treating my trauma, accepting and acknowledging my vulnerabilities, and taking better care of myself. I used to think I was doing the right thing by going flat out all the time, saying yes to every request, addressing every problem that popped up. I thought that was the way to help, but it was killing me. And if I died, I really couldn't help anyone. I had to learn to slow down, say no, eat right, find some joy, find some internal peace.

But it was a challenge. I still worried that I was missing opportunities to help; I feared I wasn't doing enough, that I was abandoning my objectives (honestly, I still do). My survivor guilt, and the lasting trauma resulting from the constant life-and-death decisions I had to take in Rwanda, caused me to fear not answering every call, running off to every event and meeting, calling back every person who wanted to interview me.

My guilt was exacerbated when I encountered strangers—usually injured vets—who demanded my time and then, if I tried to tell them that I was sorry but I couldn't meet their request this time, raged (privately and publicly) that I just didn't care enough. Eventually, though, I was forced to acknowledge that just like in a plane crash, where you have to put your own oxygen mask on before you help your child, if I took care of myself first, I could actually accomplish more. Compare the image of a cup of water that is constantly being drained to one that is always overflowing. My goal now is to try to assist others with my overflow, rather than run on empty.

I'm not always successful. I just checked my calendar, and next month I'm scheduled to speak at meetings and events in

Ontario, Quebec, Saskatchewan and Nova Scotia, as well as Rwanda, Bosnia and Herzegovina, and Ukraine (fortunately, the last one is virtual). But for the first time in my life, I have also scheduled time for myself. Time to sit still with my family, to take long walks, to discuss ideas, to read and think.

I have also learned to trust that the projects we are building—at the Dallaire Institute for Children, Peace and Security, at La fondation Roméo Dallaire, at the Montreal Institute for Genocide and Human Rights Studies, at the Dallaire Centre of Excellence for Peace and Security at the Canadian Armed Forces, at Laval University with its leadership chair, Le projet de CLÉ Roméo Dallaire sur les conflits civils et la paix durable, at Wounded Warriors Canada, along with my work with my wife on the new *Leadership Bienveillant* philosophy, and various other organizations and initiatives—will be sustained beyond my lifespan.

This has made me much less frantic, less prone to reach for the reactive duct-tape solutions that often make problems worse. By keeping a focus on prevention, we make panicky crisis management obsolete. And most importantly, that prevents human suffering, both personal and global.

SECURITY

This realm secure and full of gladsomeness,
Crowded with ancient people and with modern

Dante, *Paradiso*, Canto XXXI

uring my years in the military, I equated "security" with the use of force, and so it followed that "security sector actors"—meaning police, military, intelligence, paramilitary, guards and so on—needed to be armed. Then in the late 1990s, I heard about an entirely new concept called "human security," which struck me with the force of revelation.

I was truly surprised by how many more dimensions of "security" there could be. This conceptualization treated the presence of security forces as only one small part of security—really, the last resort. Human security was about so much more than freedom from conflict. It was also freedom from want and freedom from fear. It included access to clean water, housing, food and medical care, and it incorporated religious and cultural liberty, as well as protection from political instability and environmental disaster. To me, such a broad concept of security, extending to all aspects of human life, made a whole hell of a lot of sense. In fact, if we took care of all these factors, it would make the discipline I'd devoted my life to obsolete.

Throughout the United States and Canada over the past several years, activists have issued calls to "defund the police"— a reaction to the militarization of police forces and extreme abuses of power exhibited by officers against members of the public, especially Black and Indigenous people and those in mental health crises. The slogan is deliberately provocative, so much so that many people seem to miss its point. The idea is not necessarily to rid communities of police, but to focus "security" resources more broadly to meet the needs of communities (which, when left unmet, often spark situations that lead to police intervention). By reallocating a significant portion of the funds currently being spent on increasingly militarized policing, the theory is we could provide more in the way of mental health support and social services, creating a stronger social fabric. The focus is on prevention.

By addressing root issues around poverty (including education, health and equal access to opportunities), mental health (including emergency response, access to medical and psychosocial therapies, and drug and alcohol addiction supports), and systemic inequalities (including the removal of obstacles imposed because of race, gender and social class), and by refocusing the goal of police service from armed intervention to de-escalation, mediation and reconciliation, human security is achieved through prevention rather than punishment. By reallocating funding in this way, communities are much better "served and protected"—an idea hard to get across to people devoted to law-and-order rhetoric, who seem to think that hunkering down on the side of power is the way to security, when it is in fact the farthest thing from it.

Maddeningly, in every book I've read about peace, the dominant theme is power. Authors claim that financial, military, political and now data-driven informational power is the foundation of peace—that power is the deterrent force that provides global security. It's a disgustingly passé position mired in self-interest, ego and all the other failures of humanity I laid out in Part One. This desire for power is like a drug, constantly demanding more, and pushing people to greed. Such power is an instrument that establishes one group's security *over* another. Such power can never defuse and resolve issues in a permanent way; such power is far more likely to feed resentment, prolonging rather than resolving conflict.

The most obvious example of the bankruptcy of this thinking is nuclear weapons—the ultimate power as well as the ultimate threat. A country with nuclear capability has no incentive to dialogue about solutions to issues with a country that does not have a matching capability. Why bother negotiating when you can push for full advantage, regardless of how it affects other human beings?

Security based on carrying a big stick has proven ephemeral and unsustainable, vulnerable and volatile; it is actually a main source of *in*security. The concept of "human security" I adhere to does not include the exercise of power; its goal is to meet the needs of humanity. The hunger for power is a hindrance to achieving human security for all.

Perhaps security in the future will not require weapons at all; I certainly hope humanity evolves in that direction. I do think we will always need an active international organization of some kind that monitors for potential disruptions to security and early warning signs of conflict, but I'm not sure that such a body must be armed. Instead, the focus of security service members of the future could be to provide assistance where needed. Not to overwhelm and destroy enemies, but to respond to potential threats to well-being and help to resolve them. The role of the military is to protect its nation, but couldn't it achieve this by preventing disasters rather than stepping in with force after things explode? Our militaries could expand their depth of knowledge and breadth of tactics to become instruments that prevent frictions from ever devolving into discord. They might become so progressive and multifaceted that they not only prevent conflict, but also identify the root issues and eliminate the discord at its source. Security interventions could deploy people with the skills and tools to attenuate crisis, not with weapons to fight and kill.

Security in the classic sense, however, will continue to be a necessity as we move toward a new philosophical concept of what human security is. For some time into the future, we'll continue to face this dilemma of power and security being linked to bringing peace; as the world stands now, the potential that accountable, appropriate authorities will resort to necessary force to keep people safe does quell fear and create an atmosphere of stability on which all the other practical and philosophical steps toward peace can be built.

Many people feel the opposite of safe when dealing with security forces. As a one-time senior member of a security force myself, I know that many of us on the other side of violent encounters also bear scars (physical, mental and moral). Perhaps, then, we need to drop the term *security forces* altogether in favour of new words for the mechanism that will provide human and planetary security, and serenity, in the future.

Security and peace of mind based in profound trust is a critical, foundational component of The Peace. So much so that there can't be individual peace without such security. And there can't be world peace without global security.

INTEGRATION

A s a leader, I've always sought input from a wide variety of experts, promoted the benefits of linguistic diversity, and welcomed contributions and advice from people with experiences different from my own. In Rwanda, I was shocked to see how the disparate groups working on a shared goal failed entirely to work together. Humanitarians, diplomats, NGOs and local community organizations stuck to their own silos, refusing to communicate beyond them, an attitude that only amplified the chaos. Though most organizations were staffed by brave people doing their best to help, they maintained a dogmatic devotion to what they viewed as their independence and neutrality, even at the expense of the people they were there to assist.

NGOs, for instance, would make deals to bring humanitarian aid into the country, but belligerents wouldn't let the aid workers enter controlled territories. So they would agree to distribute the supplies meant for internally displaced civilians on the NGO's behalf, skimming a good portion for their own use. If the NGOs had agreed to work with me to deliver that aid, all of it would have reached the intended recipients. But in order to maintain their independence from a UN mission, the aid workers were willing to tolerate the skimming as an acceptable loss—a tax, as it were, on their business. They didn't appreciate that they were sustaining the conflict by allowing these supplies to slip into the hands of combatants. Out of a stubborn unwillingness to work with others, they agreed to something that was not only wrong, but also entirely against their mission of aid and of neutrality.

We did make efforts to agree on priorities and join forces in Rwanda. But some felt medical care was the top need, some urged a ceasefire, some said the biggest goal was to maintain schooling for children, and some were most worried about containing costs. I tried my best to encourage what are called the 3Cs: coordination, co-operation and collaboration.

But co-operation is highly dependent on goodwill and individual personalities. (Dr. James Orbinski, the country lead for Médecins Sans Frontières during the genocide, and I worked exceptionally well together and were able to create a protected operating hospital that saved thousands of lives.) I also found that if groups did manage to come to an agreement, it was often vetoed by their HQ "back home" (that is, thousands of miles away and often on an entirely different continent, where procedural and financial concerns took precedence over the challenges we were facing in the field).

Collaboration generally happened only when one group needed another, for instance if an NGO wanted to borrow UNAMIR trucks to deliver food aid from the airport, without the visual of peacekeepers driving them.

And coordination was, frankly, almost impossible. The meetings I held to try to get us all on the same page felt eternal—stretching for as long as eight to ten hours—yet no agreement came out of them.

One NGO from Norway did attempt to serve as a coordinating hub when multiple NGOs began to return to Rwanda after the worst of the killing was over. It was an excellent premise and it worked moderately well, except that the NGOs still regarded security forces and diplomats as secondary to their efforts, even though we were all still in a war zone.

I understand that NGOs have long-standing frictions with military forces, usually because resource distribution in a conflict zone often favours military needs over humanitarian. But this mistrustful attitude—on all sides—needs to change, everywhere. There were over seven thousand NGO personnel in Afghanistan, but NATO and US Forces commander General David Petraeus said he never spent one moment with any of them, because they didn't want to speak to him. These organizations continue to work in competition with each other, especially when playing to the media to ensure high visibility and future funding. Similarly, the military doctrine in humanitarian missions (termed "winning hearts and minds") often conflicts with NGO assessments of the needs. And far too often, chasms separate aid efforts from the communities they wish to serve. How many times have well-meaning groups built community theatres when the community actually needed clean water? The countryside of Central Africa is littered with such abandoned white elephants.

When institutions aim for multidisciplinary (or transdisciplinary or interdisciplinary) approaches to solve problems, they are on the right track. I picture it like a Rubik's cube: not only matching the colours on the six faces of the cube, but also aligning a variety of different solutions beneath the surface. That internal diversity is essential to the success of an integrated effort.

Integration, then, isn't just diverse groups finding ways to work together. Ideally, it would entail developing an entirely new system that can progress well beyond what we can achieve at present; it would likely not utilize existing mechanics (like military hierarchies, academic disciplines, or humanitarian organizations as they are currently formulated), but materialize from a new perspective.

How can these well-intentioned and important threads be woven together? Well, dialogue is a major first step—not just preaching to the choir, but engaging with a diversity of life experiences, education, training, skills and cultural awareness. To illustrate, the Dallaire Institute's Africa Centre of Excellence held a daylong session that brought together women from security forces with community women's groups that are working to stop the recruitment and use of children in armed conflict. Of course, there was discomfort on both sides at first: the community leaders were wary of the police and military members, and the women from the forces were apprehensive about speaking freely with members of the community. But once all the women realized they were working toward the same goal—to protect children—they began openly sharing ideas about how to end the recruitment of child soldiers and put a stop to gender-based violence.

Before the consultation, one of the local women leaders reported that they often had challenges approaching other communities to discuss such issues at the local level because security would block them from entering. After her eye-opening dialogue with women from the security sector, she said her new understanding of military and police procedure, and her new perspective on their roles, gave her confidence to negotiate access, and that she also now knew who to speak to at what level in the military. A small but significant example of success in integrating different players, with far-reaching results.

I would love to see a new model of integrated, multidisciplinary response that would include the participation of diverse voices, especially of women and especially of local community members (not just "experts" from Geneva and New York), allowing for input from a wide range of perspectives to come up with timely and relevant solutions to crisis situations. (This is the route that Principles for Peace, for one, is successfully taking by holding stakeholder platforms in communities around the world.) Such a response would consider all the factors and history affecting situations, cultures and regions, and ensure appropriate, multi-faceted engagement. I don't need to repeat the consequences that division and separation had on the people of Rwanda.

The lodestar of integration has been garnering attention in a variety of fields. In academia, for instance, there is a new focus on intersectionality—considering where issues around a single topic overlap, so the complex interactions can be better understood. In the field of medicine, physicians, psychologists and psychiatrists are coming together to treat veterans with operational stress injuries with a holistic care model. (It always made me chuckle that my psychiatrist would give me pills to stop my nightmares, when my psychologist needed to analyze my dreams.) In business, there has been a recent rapid uptake of policies affirming and working toward diversity, equity and inclusion (DEI). In the political realm, there has been more attention on "whole of government" solutions; Canada, for instance, created a mission made up of over ten federal departments (including Public Safety, Environment, Defence, Development and so on) that permitted government decision makers to adjust and reinforce our efforts on the ground in Afghanistan. And in international affairs, inclusion, plurality and subsidiarity, concepts that engage a diversity of voices (especially those of women, youth and local communities), are much more often on the table. Each of these ideas shares a fundamental principle: it respects human beings as unique individuals with equally valid and relevant lives and experiences.

This new attitude goes so much farther than the old concept of "tolerance." Respect for (rather than tolerance of) each other's differences is the only way to true unity; it takes away power from the masculine, the monied, the bloated, the armed, in favour of the whole community. Such innovation, however contested, is long overdue.

I don't know what will get us over this particular hump, or what integration will eventually look like, but I hope we are moving toward finding out. Surely we can discover a more altruistic driver of innovation and human behaviour than the profit motive.

By allowing us the opportunity to better understand more perspectives and lived realities, integration also breeds empathy. And empathy is a quality that really can transform the world, one person at a time.

LEXICON

Not in vague phrase . . .

But with clear words and unambiguous language

Dante, *Paradiso,* Canto xvii

Having seen, over my lifetime, what the world has called *peace*, I feel we need a word that includes far more than merely the abeyance of war. True and lasting peace must include security as we have newly defined it: freedom from fear, freedom from harm, freedom from want. How can humanity or any subgroup thereof be truly at peace if they risk starvation, for example? To quote my fellow P4P commissioner Rory Stewart, "You cannot eat peace."

But all my attempts to come up with a new word to capture this complex idea have been inadequate to the task, portmanteaus that will not carry the weight. So for the purposes of finding a title for this book, as well as for my overarching aim, I decided on *The Peace*. It's a subtle change, but I hope it sends a clear signal that I am looking at something *more* from the ideal of "peace" than its current use as a camouflage for truce.

Words, and their meanings, can hold enormous significance. In the military, we used specific action verbs in command, such as *advance, withdraw, attack, engage, deploy, disrupt* and *defend*. They are immediately recognized and understood by all service members, as well as by diplomats, nations and other global players. These are words to apply in worst-case scenarios; behind each of them is a set of procedures, tactics, metrics, doctrine, weapons, policies and training that dictate the ways to implement the action.

The trouble is, since the end of the Cold War, conflict and peace operations have drastically changed and they require a new lexicon to guide them. When you are legally and ethically responsible for putting lives on the line, it is essential to use action verbs precisely. Since the 1990s, new verbs have arisen in humanitarian and peacekeeping missions, such as *resolve, constrain, anticipate, adapt* and *protect*. But they have no mutually understood doctrine to back them up; for a military commander, they fail to communicate the parameters and direction of the mission. And that's dangerous.

This badly understood new humanitarian lexicon fails peacemakers as well as victims of conflict. New circumstances clearly do need new action verbs, but the ones we choose to use also need formal definitions and procedures, tactics, metrics, doctrine, weapons, policies and training behind them.

Even now, I find that hierarchical military language comes out of my mouth more often than I'd like. In a recent phone call with Canada's governor general, Mary Simon, in which we were discussing the plethora of Indigenous languages across our country and how they might better serve the lexicon of peace, I heard myself say, "Excellency, you are dead on target!" Once an artillery man, in some ways always an artillery man.

I think humanity is ready to update and advance its thinking, but to do so we need new well-understood, well-defined terms that illuminate new objectives. And, as I was discussing when it came to Indigenous concepts for unity, we might need to integrate words and phrases from a variety of languages.

The nuance in the way a language reflects the experiences of the particular culture it evolved in can provide significant additional meaning to an otherwise simple word. For instance, a *pâtisserie* is not the same as a bakery; blizzards, flurries, powder, whiteout, flakes, drifts, sleet, slush, squall and the white stuff are all English terms we use in Canada to describe particular incarnations of snow. A lot of beautiful and valuable concepts exist in polysynthetic languages, wherein words can be composed of many parts that each have an independent meaning. These words are often thoughtfully descriptive—as in the German for light bulb, *Glühbirne*, which literally translates as "glow pear," or the Afrikaans for stapler, which is *papier vampier* ("paper vampire").

With more than seven thousand languages spoken in the world today, the literal, implied and cultural nuances of words in translation are often lost. Terms we hope to apply universally—especially for global peace efforts—have got to meet the cultural references of those who will be using them. They shouldn't be drawn from a dominant language, such as English, because that might confuse people who are not native speakers, exacerbating tensions.

The UN operates in six official languages (Arabic, Chinese, English, French, Russian and Spanish), but primarily uses English. Documents are generally drafted in English, then

translated into the other languages. As such, English termi-
nology dominates. When the Security Council was debating
language around violence against women during one of the
1995 Beijing Conference follow-ons, the word *gender* was hotly
contested by Arabic-speaking delegations, because Arabic
makes no distinction between the concepts of "sex" and "gender." This was obviously more than just a linguistic issue, but
a cultural, religious and political one as well. English-speaking
delegates insisted that the word *sex* limits people (especially
women) to their reproductive function, as opposed to their
larger and far more complex social roles. This argument, of
course, has expanded rapidly since, as issues around gender
become better understood and the debates more nuanced,
expanding definitions far beyond the binary of ♀ and ♂.

If only we were all as clever as my African colleagues and
friends, most of whom speak upwards of six languages as a
matter of course. With that level of multilingualism, imagine what a rich lexicon we'd have to draw on. To hear these
friends converse, jumping from English to French to Swahili
to Kinyarwanda in order to use the language that best suits
the particular idea being expressed, is truly inspirational.
Though I speak and write primarily in English, a language
I feel I've reasonably mastered, I am still influenced in my
thinking when I feel there is a French word that would better
meet the meaning I wish to express. One language, like one
point of view, is limiting and can be insufficient to capture all
our thoughts and ideas.

Of course, any new word's definition needs to be clear and
the usage consistent for the message to carry. As I mentioned

earlier, in the artillery regiment I commanded, my troops were all francophone, but we were not allowed to issue fire orders in French. This would have been a surmountable problem if the orders had been in plain English. But phrases like "rounds fired for effect" and "check firing" were more challenging to unpack, especially for a non-native speaker in the fog of war. To someone with limited English, *round* means "circle" (not unit of ammunition). *Check* means "examine" (not stop).

When we are communicating globally, trying to put all our ideas into English will never reflect the appropriate depth of meaning and understanding we need to deal with the tensions between us. This doesn't mean everyone has to become fluent in several languages (though it is wonderful to try). But keeping an open mind and seeking new knowledge from diverse cultures, languages and people offers valuable intellectual flexibility and may lead to the generation of new words that precisely express the complex new ideas we need.

SANS FRONTIÈRES

Outside of time,
Outside all other limits.

Dante, *Paradiso,* Canto XXIX

Let's be very clear: the era of "the other" is *over*. Sub-Saharan African, Northern European, South Asian, Middle Eastern, Hispanic, Pacific Islander, Inuit—we are all equally human and equally worthy and deserving. We are one human race. One family.

Happily, today's young people truly have the potential to be a generation *sans frontières*—without borders—and many of them seem to understand this almost instinctively. Their comfort with internet technology has literally brought the world into the palms of their hands, and as a result, they are planetary, truly global thinkers. Though there are many regimes dedicated to getting in the way of this generational revolution, there are also young people on the streets looking for progressive change. Unless otherwise influenced by self-interested adults, these youth have the ability and the will to see humanity as a single entity connected to a singular, fragile and beautiful world.

Part of the beauty of integrating different languages into our own is that they enhance ideas in wonderful ways. *Génération sans frontières* translates as "generation without borders," but in French it also means "generation without *limits*." Which is apt: today's youth are living in an increasingly borderless world, not just when it comes to geopolitics, but also in their thinking and being. Of course, being aware of every horror happening in real time, from climate catastrophes to humanitarian ones, can weigh heavily on us all, and can lead to despair. I remember when youth were so concerned about nuclear war that they didn't want to bring children into the world; some young people today have responded to the climate crisis in the same way.

However, I believe if we follow all our other lodestars, over time we can overcome the evil and negativity in these old tools and systems. The upside can already be seen in the international followings that have coalesced around young leaders such as Greta Thunberg and Malala Yousafzai.

While some countries—Canada, the United Kingdom and the United States among them—are dealing with aging populations and all the stagnation that can signal, recent numbers from the UN confirm that the African region has the world's youngest population. By 2075, the number of youth in Africa will surpass that in India and China combined. Currently about 45 percent of the continent's population is fourteen and under. In sub-Saharan Africa, 70 percent are under thirty. These youth likely don't know it, but they hold the balance of power in their hands.

Today, young people can coalesce in the millions in real time; the power of that nascent technology is limitless. We have already seen examples of young people using their numbers and their mastery of communications to effect change. Recent movements like Black Lives Matter, Idle No More, Y'en a Marre, Red Hand Day, Me Too and Skolstrejk för klimatet have unearthed long-standing systemic problems and addressed the rage brewing at the source. They have shown the bravery and influence that previously marginalized groups, especially youth, can muster when they have a focus, especially now that they are able to come together with far-flung peers.

The huge potential for youth activism is still untapped. Some of the new generation are lost in the reflective mirrors of social media; some simply do not know how to take a first step; some have been signed up to the system imposed by previous generations, which values making money more than making change. Yet this generation, as a whole, is equipped like no other to break the mould, to shift the social imperative away from working to survive to insisting that all humans have a fair chance to thrive and live within the tenets of human rights for all.

As Barack Obama put it in 2020, addressing a young audience, "Earlier generations had to be persuaded that everyone has equal worth. For you, it's a given—a conviction."

The growing youth bulge is a great source of potential energy and ideas. Masai Ujiri, the humanitarian and founder of Giants of Africa and president of the Raptors NBA basketball team, has made it his mission to reframe how the world sees the youth of Africa, saying that while charity and aid are well and good, "Africa has *talent* and what it needs is *investment*." Today's leaders must nurture and encourage that potential, because youth numbers (their voices and their votes), their savvy and empathy, their energy, their limitless power to coalesce through technology and their global perspective give them more ability to make significant change than any generation that has come before them.

Believe me, belligerents around the world understand the value of youth. They have already recognized the enormous untapped energy of children and young adults. I saw it as long as thirty years ago in Rwanda, when most of the killings were being committed by the extremist youth militia. We see it with ISIS, al-Qaida, Boko Haram and al-Shabab; we have witnessed the ease with which both Russian and Ukrainian forces recruited children and youth into battle; and we know of innumerable street gangs and organized criminal syndicates that mobilize—no, *rely on*—indoctrinated children to do the dirty work for ruthless adults. In fact, in almost every conflict in the world today, child soldiers are used as weapons of war.

This is the temptation: for corrupt adults to take advantage of youth's eagerness to engage and participate in *anything* meaningful, particularly youth who are disenfranchised and have no other options. Young people bring incredible energy to any movement. How is it that the bad guys have picked up on this, but the good guys haven't? I believe that my country, for example, can and should find ways to energize and guide youth toward a unified and just future. It was young people who settled and built what would become Canada in the nineteenth century: 56 percent of the population in 1851 was under the age of nineteen. Sixty or so years later, it was youth who fought and died at Vimy Ridge in the First World War. Imagine if today's young people were to make similar commitments to the cause of humanity and peace.

I have noticed that young Canadians no longer seem to be going en masse to Europe, the way my generation did, to do the grand tour or the backpacking trek, paying homage to what the West built on the backs of others. No, they are now visiting the countries that are the future, in Asia, in Africa, in Latin America. They want to be on the front lines of the future.

What would happen if wealthy nations established a formal rite of passage after high school—if, going forward, every young person ended up with a pair of boots under their bed that had been soiled in the earth of a region far from their own. Before moving on with the rest of their lives, what if they had seen for themselves—touched, smelled, tasted, heard and otherwise experienced—what is happening to their global peers.

Similarly, I think democracies should also lower the voting age to sixteen. That point in adolescence is about the time youth begin to discover the wider world around them and wish to engage with it. In Canada, pretty recently, you could join the military at sixteen; with parental permission, you still can. That is also the recruitment age in most democracies. It is outrageous that adults might train troops who are not considered old enough to vote to fight wars. There is something deeply wrong with a process in which those who have the least say might end up making the largest sacrifice. This is the kind of flawed and limited thinking that the *générations sans frontières* are rejecting.

Both in the field and at home, young people can help us all reimagine how we see peace and how we see the world. Peace that exists only within our own borders is not peace; peace is achieved when all of us, everywhere, are at peace. I hope today's youth are still inspired by the words of Nelson Mandela, who said, "The future belongs to our youth. . . . They must seek and cherish the most basic condition for peace, namely unity in our diversity, and find lasting ways to that goal."

Youth today have grown up with the image of our little blue ball of a planet in all its vulnerability and unity. As astronaut Bruce McCandless pointed out, you cannot see political boundaries from space. You can't see them online either, nor on the ground; young people today have the capacity to understand that their home is not just their own backyard, town or country, but the whole planet. Such a perspective means they won't put up with some areas thriving while others flounder. They can and will demand fairness and equity, whether it is access to clean water, education or freedom from violent conflict.

Les générations sans frontières are free of the influence of a bipolar, enemy-focused past. They have grown up with the internet, the euro, the African Union. Many of them have already rejected the past's hierarchies, unbreachable boundaries and "norms." They understand, all too well, the global effects of the Anthropocene, but I think they are mostly confident in their own influence and creativity. They have an entrepreneurial, engaged, experimental, self-driven spirit that understands its own potential.

The older generation has got to get out of their way and delegate decision-making and risk-taking to them. Even though they are inexperienced, their apprenticeship in the world has been so much more far-reaching than in my day. Those of us with our hands on the levers of power have to stop asking youth to sit as tokens on the councils of their elders; we need them as full-fledged decision makers. I feel we are truly in a gestation period of activism that can be nurtured and pushed to revolutionary levels in the name of and with the ambition of humanity finding The Peace.

There is no limit to what the generations without borders can achieve.

JUSTICE

Herein doth living Justice sweeten so
Affection in us, that for evermore
It cannot warp to any iniquity.

Dante, *Paradiso*, Canto VI

More than an instrument of the law, justice is fundamental to humanity, and an absolute in the universe
of The Peace.

Wherever it prevails, justice creates a tangible atmosphere of fairness. When the International Criminal Court
held its tribunal in Sierra Leone, where the atrocities committed during that country's civil war had taken place, the population reported that they felt justice permeating their nation.
This was a far cry from the impact of the court's decision to
hold its tribunal on the 1994 genocide in Tanzania; by doing
so, it distanced Rwandan survivors from justice, which they
needed to witness being done on their soil, in their communities, in their daily lives.

As a consequence, after the perpetrators returned to their
communities to live among the victims of their crimes, Rwanda
reinvigorated a once-prevalent style of justice called *Inkiko
Gacaca*—loosely translated as "courts in the grass where

people gather"—to provide local healing through truth and reconciliation. Such courts dated to the times when the *mwami* (king) would mediate disputes and restore harmony by holding hearings in the places where the frictions arose. Gacacas waned during the period of colonization, but they were a sensible solution after the genocide. The ICC tribunal was able to go after the leaders (about ninety were indicted and sixty-one convicted), but the tiny country's own courts couldn't possibly process the hundreds of thousands who had carried out the killing. In most cases, such individuals eventually returned to their communities to participate in the Gacaca courts and reconcile with their fellow Rwandans.

Similarly, truth and reconciliation commissions in South Africa, Canada and elsewhere have provided formal opportunities for victims of injustice to be heard and the full extent of the violations against them to be revealed. The goal of these efforts, for better or for worse, is less about punishment and more about acknowledgement.

Still, for the Interahamwe who came home, there were few opportunities to deal with the trauma of their own actions— the complex guilt of having committed atrocities as a child, urged on by trusted adults, media and government. Their reintegration into the day-to-day life of Rwandan society has been difficult for the victims and their families. But it has also been hard for these former members of the youth militia. The challenge for all parties is to build trust in each other again.

Justice is a complicated notion to formalize; for one thing, there is no universal agreement on how to address injustice.

Do we punish criminals or reform them? Seek an eye for an eye or turn the other cheek? Our justice system in Canada asks us to abide by established rules and punishes us when we don't. But even when we think the laws are clear, who's guilty and who's innocent can be highly contentious.

Omar Khadr was born in 1986 in Toronto. His parents were both Canadian citizens who had immigrated from Pakistan. The family travelled back and forth between Canada and Pakistan throughout Khadr's young life, eventually moving to Afghanistan when Khadr was ten, when his father (an active member of al-Qaida) began NGO work there. In the aftermath of the 9/11 attacks, American soldiers became involved in a short firefight with Afghan fighters at the residential complex where Khadr's family lived. The fifteen-year-old was home at the time, and he ended up being shot in the back by an American soldier. Blinded in one eye and with two massive holes through his chest, Khadr was carried away by the soldiers to receive medical treatment. After he regained consciousness days later, he was kept from returning home or communicating with his family, interrogated and tortured for weeks (the Americans claim the techniques used on the boy were legal), and Khadr eventually confessed under duress to throwing the hand grenade that killed an American soldier during the firefight. He was transferred without trial to the Guantanamo Bay prison in Cuba, where he was held for eight years under horrific conditions. When he was asked by an American psychologist in 2010 what he missed most about his pre-incarceration life, Khadr, then twenty-three, responded, "Being loved."

Serving in the Canadian Senate at the time, I passionately advocated for Canada to bring him home, but Prime Minister Stephen Harper and his government insisted Khadr was a terrorist and a criminal. They simply refused to acknowledge that his age during that firefight made him a child soldier under the Convention on the Rights of the Child and the Optional Protocol on the involvement of children in armed conflict, which Canada not only signed but helped create.

In 2012, the government was at last convinced to allow Khadr to be transferred to a Canadian jail, where he remained until 2015. After he was released, he lived under strict bail conditions until 2019, when a Canadian judge ruled that thirty-three-year-old Omar Khadr could live as a free man.

Khadr's case, which seems so clearly unjust to me, was one of the most contentious and divisive in our country's history. There is *no* question that he was a child at the time of the incident. There are *many* questions about how his "confession" was obtained. There is *no* question that every nation on Earth had signed the Convention on the Rights of the Child, which defines a child as any person under the age of eighteen. (The United States remains the only country in the world not to ratify the convention.) The innumerable human rights violations at Guantanamo Bay—the UN described the prison as "a site of unparalleled notoriety, defined by the systematic use of torture, and other cruel, inhuman or degrading treatment against hundreds of men brought to the site and deprived of their most fundamental rights"—are *unquestionable*, but no one has ever been held accountable. And while there is *no* question that according to its own rule of law, the Canadian government of the time failed to protect Khadr, some people were irate when he received a $10.5 million settlement as compensation for what had happened to him. Addressing such concerns, Prime Minister Justin Trudeau noted that rights and freedoms must be upheld, "whether you agree with them or not," and that those who were angry about the payout should also be angry "when a government violates a Canadian, any Canadian's, fundamental rights, and allows them to be tortured."

In 1968, Justin Trudeau's father declared that Canada must aspire to be a "just society." He meant so much more than the simple application of laws; he was making a call for fairness and equality for all Canadians. Where both Trudeaus focused on justice, the man who held the prime minister's office during the Khadr years, Stephen Harper, was more concerned with making Canada "safe," as he defined it. To achieve this, he was "tough on crime," deliberately and aggressively holding criminals accountable for their misdeeds, and restricting judges' ability to contextualize the crimes or consider mitigating circumstances.

Too often, people consider justice best served by cold impartiality and rigid legality: crime and fitting punishment. But an environment of justice is loftier than the application of the rule of law and the meting out of punishment. I hope one day humanity will create a system to deal with injustice that doesn't *impose* injustice. The lodestar to aim for here is a vision of justice that embraces fairness, equality, rightness and trust.

That is the kind of justice that will breed the certainty and serenity that is as essential to humanity as love. I believe that relating to each other and our planet justly, with respect, empathy and humility, will create the confidence that allows us to take the final leap toward The Peace.

THE PEACE

O joy! O gladness inexpressible!
O perfect life of love and peacefulness!
O riches without hankering secure!

Dante, *Paradiso*, Canto XXVII

W hen Dante reaches the final sphere in *The Divine Comedy*, he learns that it is not the end. Instead, it is his point of departure on the journey toward his real destination, which he names the Empyrean. He doesn't tell us more about it because he can't: the transcendence he envisions is beyond even that great poet's extraordinary imagination.

This is what The Peace has come to mean to me: it is the as-yet-indescribable place from which we can begin to reckon with our true potential in the universe. When I first set out to write this book, my goal was to come up with strategic solutions for our present-day purgatory—a new conceptual framework for conflict prevention. But I've gone from thinking about how to get us to The Peace to thinking about how to get us *beyond* it. I picture The Peace not only as a state without suffering, but as a state so secure it will allow us the room to contemplate and even realize our true potential as human beings. I figure if we manage to achieve and sustain The Peace, an even higher objective, currently obscured from us, might come into view.

I've already warned you that this journey I've been on has become a spiritual quest. A crucial one, in my view. Humanity is on the precipice of great change. Technological advance is our carrot, environmental disaster is our stick, and the limitless, borderless thinking of the newest generations has the potential to be our awakening. I've come to this recognition not just through spiritual belief, but also through my lived experience. I have literally gone through hell, spent years in purgatory, and now, to this old soldier's astonishment, I find myself on a completely unfamiliar and serene plane of existence—truly, a kind of paradise. The ethos and purpose I had as a military man, as a senator and as a humanitarian was important, but it was still too limited. I am now embarked on a journey that is revealing itself to me at the same time as it is being created by me. But because I am actually living it each day (as I had lived in those other, darker realms, for so very long), I feel I can say that if we truly want to aim for The Peace, this pathway is achievable, if not easy.

Even if you have no desire to walk with me, I hope you agree that we desperately need to move away from the values that have given us the greedy Opulencene we currently inhabit (which also sustains horrific poverty) to a world that prioritizes the care and stewardship of the Earth and all its inhabitants. Our consciousness, our sustaining planet, our miraculous existence (whether by fluke or design) is a gift. And perhaps in time, we may strive beyond ourselves to consider what we can contribute, not just here on Earth, but also to the cosmos. By this, I don't mean sending people in rockets to other planets in literal acts of exploration, but tuning our consciousness so that we're not simply floating in space, passengers on our little rock, but part of the universe. We are made of stardust, after all.

Does humanity exist just to sustain itself? Or is there something more? From a very dark place in which I saw the worst of what humans can do to other humans, I've come to a point in life where I believe the answer is more than mere survival.

I remember one of my last visits with my mother, who was fading away with Alzheimer's. We were sitting on the patio of her old folks' home, a newspaper unopened beside us, as the first stars appeared in the night sky. I asked if she thought there were other beings out there in the universe with intelligence and creativity and feelings like ours. She was a very religious person, and her immediate, emphatic response was, No, that would be impossible. God only created humans. All that space out there beyond our atmosphere was of no consequence; to her, there was nothing in the universe but us and God.

I simply cannot conceive that atoms and gases came together to create humanity in a one-time accident. I wonder if the universe *is* the God my mother had such faith in. If we believe in a higher being, or even if we don't, the universe continues to expand. It is thriving. It is limitless. And it should be an example for us.

My mother's perspective represents to me where we currently are: insecure, desperate to sustain ourselves in wilful ignorance, dealing with constant struggle, friction and isolation.

I hear too much cynical survivalism being spouted every-where—arguments that humanity is finite, that the planet and its sun will come to an end. Why are we willing to accept that premise? Even if it is a reality, or even a possibility, to focus on annihilation as the inevitable future will condemn us to a perpetual purgatory.

At least if we can advance toward The Peace, we can spend our energy on possibilities. Then our future will depend on us to go beyond the limits, toward our bigger raison d'être. I believe that aiming for The Peace will emancipate us, turning us away from simple survival toward a potential that we haven't even considered and that we can't yet imagine. Something we can create, beyond ourselves, that could reach to the stars. A *feu sacré* feeding still-to-be-discovered entities, like the sun has fed us for millennia.

This is my real message. Achieving The Peace is ultimately not a goal of self-interest, but a way to harness our extraordinary potential to give—to radiate energy out into the universe. That energy, I believe, is *love*, a word I learned the value of so late in life. For, as Dante ends his magnum opus, it is *Love which moves the sun and the other stars.*

FURTHER READING

Allen, John. *Rabble-Rouser for Peace: The Authorized Biography of Desmond Tutu.*

Allen, Susan, and Amy Yuen. *The Politics of Peacekeeping: UN Security Council Oversight across Peacekeeping Missions.*

Appiah, Kwame Anthony. *The Lies That Bind: Rethinking Identity.*

Aspen Institute Conference on International Peace and Security. *Managing Conflict in the Post–Cold War World: The Role of Intervention.*

Autesserre, Séverine. *The Frontlines of Peace: An Insider's Guide to Changing the World.*

Barnett, Michael. *Eyewitness to a Genocide: The United Nations and Rwanda.*

Bass, Gary Jonathan. *Stay the Hand of Vengeance: The Politics of War Crimes Tribunals.*

Beardsley, Kyle, and Holger Schmidt. "Following the Flag or Following the Charter?: Examining the Determinants of UN Involvement in International Crises, 1945–2002." *International Studies Quarterly.*

Benson, Michelle, and Colin Tucker. "The Importance of UN Security Council Resolutions in Peacekeeping Operations." *Journal of Conflict Resolution*.

Boniface, Pascal. *The Will to Powerlessness: Reflections on Our Global Age*.

Cederman, Lars-Erik, and Yannick Pengl. *Global Conflict Trends and Their Consequences*.

Chalk, Frank, Roméo Dallaire, et al. *Mobilizing the Will to Intervene: Leadership to Prevent Mass Atrocities*.

Chesterman, Simon, Michael Ignatieff, and Ramesh Thakur, eds. *Making States Work: State Failure and the Crisis of Governance*.

Cohen, Eliot A. *The Big Stick: The Limits of Soft Power and the Necessity of Military Force*.

Cooper, Robert. *The Breaking of Nations: Order and Chaos in the Twenty-First Century*.

Cortright, David. *Peace: A History of Movements and Ideas*.

Dante Alighieri. *The Divine Comedy* (translation by Henry Wadsworth Longfellow).

David, Charles-Philippe. *La guerre et la paix: Approches et enjeux de la sécurité et de la stratégie*.

Dempsey, Martin, and Ori Brafman. *Radical Inclusion: What the Post-9/11 World Should Have Taught Us About Leadership*.

Duclert, Vincent. *France, Rwanda and the Tutsi—Genocide (1990-1994)—Report submitted to the President of the Republic on 26 March, 2021*

Einsiedel, Sebastian von, et al. "Civil War Trends and the Changing Nature of Armed Conflict." United Nations University Occasional Paper.

Ferguson, Niall. *The War of the World: Twentieth-Century Conflict and the Descent of the West.*

Fukuyama, Francis. "The End of History?" *The National Interest.*

Gilligan, Michael, and Stephen John Stedman. "Where Do the Peacekeepers Go?" *International Studies Review.*

Greene, Robert. *The 48 Laws of Power.*

Haggart, Blayne, and Natasha Tusikov. *The New Knowledge: Information, Data, and the Remaking of Global Power.*

Hardt, Heidi. *Time to React: The Efficiency of International Organizations in Crisis Response.*

Henripin, Jacques. *Les défis d'une population mondiale en déséquilibre.*

Homer-Dixon, Thomas. *The Upside of Down: Catastrophe, Creativity, and the Renewal of Civilization.*

ICISS. *The Responsibility to Protect: Report of the International Commission on Intervention and State Sovereignty, 2001.*

Jones, Bruce, Carlos Pascual, and Stephen John Stedman. *Power and Responsibility: Building International Order in an Era of Transnational Threats.*

Kagan, Robert. *Of Paradise and Power: America and Europe in the New World Order.*

Kaldor, Mary. *New and Old Wars: Organized Violence in a Global Era.*

Kant, Immanuel. *Perpetual Peace.*

Kuhn, Thomas S. *The Last Writings of Thomas A. Kuhn: Incommensurability in Science.*

Leader, Joyce E. *From Hope to Horror: Diplomacy and the Making of the Rwanda Genocide.*

McEwen, Haley, and Lata Narayanaswamy. "The International Anti-Gender Movement." United Nations Research Institute for Social Development.

McKee, James A. *Synaptic Fireflies: Reflections on the Meaning of Life.*

Melvern, Linda. *Conspiracy to Murder: The Rwandan Genocide.*

———. *Intent to Deceive: Denying the Genocide of the Tutsi.*

Monteiro, Nuno P. "Unrest Assured: Why Unipolarity Is Not Peaceful." *International Security.*

Murray, Williamson, and Jim Lacey, eds. *The Making of Peace: Rulers, States, and the Aftermath of War.*

Muse, Robert F. *A Foreseeable Genocide: The Role of the French Government in Connection with the Genocide against the Tutsi in Rwanda.*

Neiman, Susan. *Evil in Modern Thought: An Alternative History of Philosophy.*

Off, Carol. *Bitter Chocolate: Investigating the Dark Side of the World's Most Seductive Sweet.*

Prunier, Gérard. *The Rwanda Crisis: History of a Genocide.*

Rawls, John. *A Theory of Justice.*

Slaughter, Anne-Marie. *A New World Order.*

Smith, Stephen. Dante's *Divine Comedy.* Hillsdale College online course.

Strand, Håvard, et al. *Trends in Armed Conflict, 1946–2018.*

Tugwell, Maurice. *Peace with Freedom.*

Varret, Jean (Général). *Souviens-toi: Mémoires à l'usage des générations futures.*

Wagamese, Richard. *What Comes from Spirit.*

ACKNOWLEDGEMENTS

For their always wise and generous support, I thank my team—Anne Collins, Jessica Dee Humphreys, Phil Lancaster and Alexandre Pelletier—and my coterie of *éminences grises*: Henry Anyidoho, Lloyd Axworthy, Kenneth Bartlett, Brent Beardsley, Marc-André Blanchard, Frank Chalk, Ralph Coleman, Howard Coombs, Charles-Philippe David, Gareth Evans, Nigel Fisher, Robert Fowler, Jonathan Granoff, Marius Grinius, Bernd Horn, David Hyman, Michael Ignatieff, Marie Lamarche, David Last, Don MacNeil, Kyle Matthews, Linda Melvern, Steven Moore, Walter Natynczyk, Carol Off, Al Okros, James Orbinski, Hiba Qasas, Bob Rae, Vern Redekop, Iqbal Riza, Allan Rock, Mike Rosteck, Harjit Sajjan, Joe Sharpe, Mary Simon, Stephen Smith, Jim Stanford, Ken Watkin and Shelly Whitman.

INDEX

INDEX

Q

Quebec
  FLQ crisis, 76, 81, 126
  language clash in, 73–74
  separatism in, 76, 81, 170

R

racism, 140–41. *See also* colonialism;
  disinterest; hate
  towards Africa, 40–42
  in Canada, 132
  ignorance and, 57
  in United States, 70, 76, 132
Rally for the Return of Refugees and
  Democracy to Rwanda (RDR),
  97–98
recolonization, 81
reconciliation, 225–26
refugees, 78–79, 161
  Rwandan, 37, 68, 134–35
religion. *See* Catholic Church
Renaissance, 165–68
  Italian, 165–67, 177, 178
  and peace, 167–68
  personal, 173–74
residential schools, 77–78, 132
Responsibility to Protect (R2P), 102–3,
  106, 145–50
  Canada and, 146–47
revenge, 89–94
revolution, 153–64
  climate change as, 159–62
  in human rights, 155–56
  Renaissance as, 165, 167
  against social institutions, 156–59
  in technology, 153–55
RGF (Rwandan Government Forces),
  29, 31, 55
rights. *See* human rights
Rock, Allan, 147
Rohingya people, 78, 102
RPF (Rwandan Patriotic Front), 17,
  21–22, 30, 34. *See also* Kagame, Paul
  Uganda and, 35–36, 48
RTLM (Hutu radio station), 18, 21,
  67–68, 69–70, 97

Russia, 5, 6, 47, 92–93, 149
  and Syria, 56, 102
  Ukraine invasion, 5, 6–7, 92, 93, 102,
  104, 151
Rwanda, 142, 170–71. *See also*
  Rwandan genocide
  Arusha Accords, 17, 34, 45, 58, 61
  Belgium and, 16, 29–30, 41–42, 47,
  62–63, 65–67
  Canada and, 48, 49
  colonialism and, 62–63, 65–66, 79–80
  and Congo, 102
  disinterest in, 39, 40–42, 51–53,
  140–41
  ignorance about, 26, 28–29, 57, 58,
  59–60, 61–62
  justice in, 225–26
  NGOs in, 203–5
  refugees from, 37, 134
  refugees in, 68, 134–35
  social/political structure, 62–63,
  65–67
  United Kingdom and, 29–30, 47
  United States and, 29–30, 47, 137
  UN presence in, 32–33, 68–69, 85
Rwandan genocide, 1–2, 13, 19–21. *See*
  also Hutus; Tutsis
  aftermath, 2–3, 93–94, 225–26
  atrocities, 69–71
  civilians as perpetrators, 90, 96
  civilians as targets, 19, 55, 68, 91
  colonialism as root cause, 16–17
  denial of, 95–97
  fear and, 43, 65–66, 67–69, 70–71
  France and, 29–31, 33, 36, 41–42,
  54–55
  Habyarimana and, 29–31, 33–34
  hatred as tool, 85–86
  as Hell on Earth, 13–14, 22
  Hutus and, 84–85, 97–98
  international response, 137, 203–5
  peace negotiations, 26–27, 37–38
  scope, 59, 69–70, 85–86
  United Nations and, 18–21, 26–27,
  96–97
  young people and, 220

GENERAL ROMÉO DALLAIRE is a celebrated global human rights advocate, a highly respected author, public speaker, political adviser and former Canadian senator. Throughout his distinguished military career, General Dallaire served most notably as Force Commander of the United Nations Assistance Mission for Rwanda during the 1994 genocide. He continues to work ceaselessly to bring international attention to situations too often ignored, whether the prevention of mass atrocities, ending the recruitment and use of children in armed conflict, the impact of post-traumatic stress disorder on veterans and their families, or strategic solutions for lasting peace.